"Relatable, relevant, and revitalizing. Once again, Carol has written a Bible study that brings the Word to life and transformation to your heart."

—**Pam Farrel**, author of 58 books including *Discovering Good News in John* and the best-selling *Men Are Like Waffles, Women Are Like Spaghetti*

"Our brother, the apostle Peter, wrote a timeless message to equip and encourage us, the church. And now with her passion for scripture and life-giving insights, our sister Carol highlights the relevance of Peter's words and gives us space to reflect on our Savior's calling and the hope we have in Him."

—**Amy Groeschel**, cofounder of Life.Church and founder of Branch15, a nonprofit ministry providing care to women

"This Bible study captured my heart, reminded me of how enduring scripture is, and challenged me to make important decisions about my next steps in life. Carol McLeod has the unique ability to combine deep teaching with thought-provoking exercises and poignant applications. It is impossible to do this study without being changed from the inside out."

—**Carol Kent**, founder & executive director of Speak Up Ministries, speaker & author of *When I Lay My Isaac Down*

"In her book *Timeless*, Carol McLeod guides us through the powerful truths of the book of 1 Peter. Carol walks her readers through 9 weeks of robust biblical teachings, tender moments of reflection, and practical applications of scripture. Carol reminds us that the word of God truly withstands the test of time."

—**Cassandra Speer**, best-selling author, Bible teacher, and vice president of Her True Worth

"*Timeless* is a wake-up call to remember the hope we have in Christ. Carol McLeod leads us into a deeper understanding of 1 Peter with wisdom, care, and relevance. This Bible study is both practical and pivotal in understanding how Christianity fits into our modern world. *Timeless* is a top recommendation for anyone looking to live a God-honoring life."

—**Jenny Randle**, ministry founder of Freedom Creatives and multipublished author, including *Flash Theology*

"When Carol McLeod writes, her passion for the Word of God pulsates through every phrase! *Timeless* is no exception. Join Carol, as she unpacks the book of 1 Peter. Your faith will be strengthened and your courage bolstered as you dive into this great Bible study. You're going to walk away transformed!"

—**Becky Harling**, international speaker, Bible teacher, and author of *Our Father: A six Week Study of the Lord's Prayer*

"Peter. The one who walked on water. The one who denied Jesus in his darkest moment. The one who brings us the timeless, eternal words of God in 1 Peter. Jesus called Peter 'the rock,' and through Carol's words, you will experience the Holy Spirit empowering you to stand strong in this generation."

—**Angela Donadio**, ministry leader, author, and host of *Make Life Matter* podcast

"Carol McLeod has done it again. Every time she writes a new Bible study, she unearths fresh gems of wisdom and precious nuggets of truth. The truths of God's Word are indeed timeless, and as we embrace them they change us in ways hard to imagine. Let Carol McLeod show you how through this marvelous book."

—**Ann Tatlock**, novelist, children's book author, editor, writing mentor

"Brace yourself as you read this new book, *Timeless*. It is written by one of the most insightful storytellers of our day, Carol McLeod. I found my theology challenged, and God pointedly addressed me, 'Don't read this for information; read it for transformation.' Here I am in the last quarter of my life, and God, in His mercy, sends this book to bring my thoughts in line with His. You will also be challenged."

—**Tim Cameron**, best-selling author of *The Forty-Day Word Fast* and *40 Days Through the Prayers of Jesus*

"Carol does a fantastic job of unpacking and teaching 1 Peter in a way that is both palatable and interactive. Carol presents these ancient writings in a way that is, without a doubt, relevant and deeply meaningful for us today. The format is easily digested in small daily doses of engaging truth. This is a must-read for all seeking a deeper relationship with Jesus Christ."

—**Christy Christopher**, speaker, author of *Incredible Intervention* and *Until the Day Breaks and the Shadows Flee*

"*Timeless* is a gift for women today. From start to finish, Carol pulls you into the story of 1 Peter and gives you an understanding of who Peter was and how we relate to him. Carol lovingly unpacks the complexities of 1 Peter in a way that draws you closer not only to God but also to others in your life."

—**Sarah Schieber**, speaker, top 30 Billboard singer/songwriter, author of *A Journey Called Grief*

"I loved this book! In daily doses, Carol McLeod gently leads us to examine the writings of the apostle Peter through the lens of our own thoughts and actions. It is transformative!"

—**Cheryl Weber**, cohost, *100 Huntley Street*

"In *Timeless*, Carol McLeod opens up the timeless truths of the gospel in 1 Peter. These truths are relevant yesterday, today, and in the future. Although I recommend this study for all women, it's a great tool for a new Christian in understanding the basic truths of our faith."

—**Ginny Dent Brant**, speaker and author of *Unleash Your God-Given Healing*

Timeless

The Living *and* Enduring Word of God

Carol McLeod

IRON
STREAM

Birmingham, Alabama

Timeless

Iron Stream
An imprint of Iron Stream Media
100 Missionary Ridge
Birmingham, AL 35242
IronStreamMedia.com

Copyright © 2023 by Carol McLeod

Iron Stream Media serves its authors as they express their views, which may not express the views of the publisher.

Cover design by twoline || Studio

ISBN: 978-1-56309-621-1 (paperback)
ISBN: 978-1-56309-622-8 (eBook)
1 2 3 4 5—27 26 25 24 23

CONTENTS

————— · • ◉ • · —————

INTRODUCTION

·•●•·

Is it possible for a book written nearly two thousand years ago to maintain its intrinsic and vital impact? Is there a demarcation point when literature is deemed old-fashioned or even archaic? Those are interesting questions deserving a thoughtful and wise answer.

Beowulf, the epic and heroic English poem, is known as one of the most significant pieces of Old English literature. It is believed to have been composed between 700 and 750 AD. Perhaps you would like to gaze at the first few lines of a manuscript considered by many to be the highest achievement of Old English Literature:

> Hwæt. We Gardena in geardagum,
> þeodcyninga, þrym gefrunon,
> hu ða æþelingas ellen fremedon.
> Oft Scyld Scefing sceaþena þreatum,
> monegum mægþum, meodosetla ofteah,
> egsode eorlas. Syððan ærest wearð
> feasceaft funden, he þæs frofre gebad,
> weox under wolcnum, weorðmyndum þah,
> oðþæt him æghwylc þara ymbsittendra
> ofer hronrade hyran scolde,
> gomban gyldan. þæt wæs god cyning.[1]

The renowned *Beowulf* certainly has not stood the test of time, has it? This piece of respected literature has nothing to say to the world we live in today. Now, let's look at another example.

William Shakespeare is widely regarded as the greatest writer in the English language. One would assume with such a reputation that his writings would speak to those who live in the twenty-first century. Let's read with enthusiasm Shakespeare's Sonnet 3:

> Look in thy glass and tell the face thou viewest,
> Now is the time that face should form another,

Whose fresh repair if now thou not renewest,
Thou dost beguile the world, unbless some mother.
For where is she so fair whose uneared womb
Disdains the tillage of thy husbandry?
Or who is he so fond will be the tomb
Of his self-love, to stop posterity?
Thou art thy mother's glass, and she in thee
Calls back the lovely April of her prime;
So thou through windows of thine age shalt see,
Despite of wrinkles, this thy golden time.
 But if thou live rememb'red not to be,
 Die single, and thine image dies with thee.[2]

Many of the brilliant writings of Shakespeare are impossible to comprehend in the twenty-first century without a dictionary, an advanced college course, and repeated reading.

Shakespeare wrote during the early 1600s. Perhaps we should move ahead on the timeline of literature and discern if something written about two hundred years ago might speak to our souls and intellect.

Pride and Prejudice contains a lovely story that has consistently captured the hearts of readers, though its verbiage seems bulky and outdated. I'm likely in the minority, as I can lose myself in all the *hithers* and *thithers* and *mischances* of the magnificent yet moldy novel.

It's true that even the most well-respected pieces of literature lose their impact over years and decades, altering their meaning from applicable to archaic. However, there is one timeless literary work that does exist.

Living and Enduring

The book of 1 Peter was written nearly two thousand years ago, which translates to roughly 730,000 days. Rarely does a book of that age speak to a current generation of readers. And yet, this book written 104,000 weeks ago, continues to hold great meaning and application to those who live in the twenty-first century. It is practical, hopeful, and as up-to-date as anything you might read on the internet.

These are the words Peter employs to describe the Bible as he writes to a church in persecution.

Through the living and enduring word of God. (1 Peter 1:23)

The one component that sets the Word of God apart from all other pieces of literature is the author—the Holy Spirit wrote it. The Bible is divinely inspired by the unction of the Holy Spirit and has been written on paper through the hands of ordinary men. The Bible was not penned because the men who wrote it were seasoned writers, talented wordsmiths, or possessed large vocabularies. The Bible was transcribed because the Holy Spirit spoke to and then through human beings made in the very image of God.

The words the Holy Spirit spoke two millennia ago through Peter, the rock upon which Christ would build His church, hold dynamic and intrinsic power for your life today.

As we study the book of 1 Peter, you, like Peter, will hear the unmistakable voice of the Holy Spirit. The tone and delivery of the Holy Spirit will fill your heart, your mind, and your homes if you give Him your full attention.

The Holy Spirit has always been God's selected agent of change in the lives of His children. We serve a God who never changes but He loves to observe the change the Holy Spirit inspires in the hearts of His followers. Whenever God sees a situation or a heart that needs a radical transformation, He sends the Holy Spirit to gently blow the winds of metamorphosis. You, my friend, will experience this peaceful yet persistent breeze as you study the book of 1 Peter. I hope we are all wonderfully surprised by the adjustments that happen in our thought processes, in the words we speak, the attitudes we embrace, and the actions we demonstrate directly due to the letter the apostle Peter wrote to the infant church.

The book of 1 Peter does not carry a single theme, but it addresses many issues common to every generation. Our theology will be challenged, our ethics sterilized, our doctrine repaired, and our everyday lives will be renewed by diving into this fascinating study.

This epistle carries the name of the opinionated fisherman, Peter, and is a call to holiness and humility. It presents practical wisdom for marriages, work relationships, political discourse, and evangelism. We will examine the deep mysteries of joy, faith, sorrow, trials, and God's unconditional love in this missive filled with hope.

Every Week

I hope you will commit to answering the questions found in each day's reading. These questions are meant to be purposeful as well as practical.

The Word of God often acts as a mirror when we apply the principles of Scripture to our daily walk and to our heart attitudes. As we observe our lives through the reflection of Scripture, we become more like Christ and ground our lives in His promises. Often it will prove painful to answer the questions crafted for growth and encouragement, but it is pain of the very best kind. We never mature without some type of uncomfortable stretching, and we will never change without self-examination. Therefore, at the close of each day's reading, there is a section titled, *The Mirror*. This simple reflective inquiry will assist in applying the studied scripture to your life.

I also challenge you to memorize the weekly Bible verse aptly named *Eternal Words*. The Word of God is able to guide you safely through the fiercest of storms and to protect you in the most searing of fires. I hope you will join me in the singular joy of memorizing Scripture, knowing it will carry you through anything.

Each day's reading concludes with a prayer. Please read this prayer out loud and agree with its content. There is no limitation to the power of prayer. When we pray, not only do we grab God's attention, but our hearts are always transformed in the process. I have long believed that history belongs to those who pray.

It's Time!

Now, it is time to dig into the wonder, the practical living advice, and the timeless wisdom Peter offers. This gift is not only available to the early church but also to us—those who deeply desire to serve Christ at this challenging moment in history.

Lord Jesus, I pray for every woman who is about to be undone, satisfied, and made new by the book of 1 Peter. We give You permission to challenge our thinking, to restore our vision, and to rescue our hearts from the sludge of our culture. Thank You, Father, for the Bible. We receive it as God's specific Word to us today. In Jesus' name. Amen.

Week 1

Follow Me

Day 1

Who Was Peter?

Peter, a rugged fisherman with fish guts under his fingernails and a staunch stubborn streak in his soul, was just a young man when he first met Jesus. Peter visibly carried the characteristics of youthful passion—most theologians describe this fiery fisherman as opinionated and impetuous.

Peter and his brother, Andrew, heard the voice of Jesus one day when they were casting their nets into the Sea of Galilee. Close your eyes and imagine the sound of the waves rolling upon the shore. Can you hear the wind as it blows across the water? I wonder if Jesus began His stroll along the seashore looking specifically for these two young fishermen or if He simply came upon them. I can't help but believe Peter and Andrew were chosen from the beginning of time. Their role in the plan of God had always been in the heart of Jesus.

> *Now as Jesus was walking by the Sea of Galilee, He saw two brothers, Simon who was called Peter, and Andrew his brother, casting a net into the sea; for they were fishermen.*
>
> *And He said to them, "Follow Me, and I will make you fishers of men." Immediately they left their nets and followed Him. (Matthew 4:18–20)*

Peter left *everything* to follow Jesus. He abandoned his fishing boat on the rocky shoreline and discarded his economic stability. He walked away from his former, comfortable lifestyle and chose a relationship with the One who said, "I will transform your life. I will change your focus from temporary to eternal. I will reveal to you what life is truly all about!"

Today, the Savior is still inviting men and women to obey Him and make an eternal difference in the world. The question is, will our response mirror Peter's? Will we act immediately? There was no hesitation in Peter's decision to yield to the voice of Jesus. His example may help you answer the following questions.

⧗   *What does it mean to "follow Jesus"?*

⧗   *Have you decided to follow Him?*

Jesus intentionally chose Peter as a disciple even though He was surely aware of Peter's shortcomings. Stubborn attitudes and an inability to control his mouth were issues for Peter. Jesus has also chosen you to serve Him, even though He is keenly aware of everything you are—as well as everything you are not. Jesus continues to choose the headstrong, the mouthy, and the unrefined to serve His unshakable kingdom. He equally calls the insecure, painfully shy, and obsessive-compulsive. The glaring but unavoidable truth is that imperfect people are the only type of people God uses.

⧗   *List three characteristics that describe you:*

1. _____

2. _____

3. _____

⧗   *If you could do just one thing for the Lord, what would you want to do?*

⌛ *Is there a habit or a relationship you might need to leave behind to follow Jesus?*

Peter and Me

Peter has always been my favorite disciple—likely because I see so much of myself in him. I have been known to allow my unbridled opinions to rush out of my mouth like the fierce waters of Niagara Falls. My emotions often rule my thought life, my speech patterns, as well as my behavior. I, like Peter, have the reputation of talking first and thinking later, which is never a healthy way of responding.

Peter is the disciple who asked Jesus for the power to walk upon the stormy waves of the Sea of Galilee.

> *But the boat was already a long distance from the land, battered by the waves; for the wind was contrary. And in the fourth watch of the night He came to them, walking on the sea. When the disciples saw Him walking on the sea, they were terrified, and said, "It is a ghost!" And they cried out in fear. But immediately Jesus spoke to them, saying, "Take courage, it is I; do not be afraid."*
>
> *Peter said to Him, "Lord, if it is You, command me to come to You on the water." And He said, "Come!" And Peter got out of the boat, and walked on the water and came toward Jesus. But seeing the wind, he became frightened, and beginning to sink, he cried out, "Lord, save me!" Immediately Jesus stretched out His hand and took hold of him, and said to him, "You of little faith, why did you doubt?"* **(Matthew 14:24–31)**

We are quick to blame Peter for becoming frightened and sinking in the angry waters, but never forget that he was the only disciple who responded with faith. It was Peter who said, "Jesus, I want to do what you are doing. Even in the middle of a vicious storm, call me to come to You!"

Oh, how I long for the faith of Peter even in the middle of a fierce and raging storm. I want to be the one who says, "Jesus, I want to do what you are doing!"

⧗   *What is one lesson that resonates with you as you read the account of Peter walking on the water?*

Peter is famously known for rebuking the Lord during a moment of searing heartbreak, while Jesus prepared His disciples for His future suffering and certain crucifixion. Peter's reaction to Jesus was certainly not his finest hour.

> **Peter took Him aside and began to rebuke Him, saying, "God forbid it, Lord! This shall never happen to You." (Matthew 16:22)**

Unfortunately, like Peter, I have also tried unsuccessfully and humiliatingly to rebuke the Lord. When God does not respond on my preferred time-table to my desperate prayers or He answers with a gentle but emphatic "no" or "not yet," I often grumble or whine. In my self-serving petitions, I, like Peter, have dismally reproved the Lord. At times, I tell others loudly about my disappointment concerning God's response. Ashamedly, even more often than I am guilty of verbal rebuke, I admonish the Lord in my thoughts. Can you relate?

⧗   *Has there ever been a time when you complained about the Lord, His timing, or His answers? If so, take a minute to write about it.*

⧗ *Now, perhaps you would like to write a prayer of repentance for the time when, like Peter, you chose to rebuke the Lord.*

Also, like Peter, I have been known to sleep rather than pray. Jesus took Peter, James, and John with Him to the Garden of Gethsemane the night of His arrest. Jesus knew what would transpire in the next few days and grieved to the point of death. Certainly, these men who had spent three years hearing the teachings of Jesus, observing the miracles, and experiencing His unmatched compassion would extend their faithful friendship during this night of trauma.

> *Then Jesus came with them to a place called Gethsemane, and said to His disciples, "Sit here while I go over there and pray." And He took with Him Peter and the two sons of Zebedee, and began to be grieved and distressed. Then He said to them, "My soul is deeply grieved, to the point of death; remain here and keep watch with Me."*
>
> *And He went a little beyond them, and fell on His face and prayed, saying, "My Father, if it is possible, let this cup pass from Me; yet not as I will, but as You will." And He came to the disciples and found them sleeping, and said to Peter, "So, you men could not keep watch with Me for one hour? Keep watching and praying that you may not enter into temptation; the spirit is willing, but the flesh is weak."*
>
> *He went away again a second time and prayed, saying, "My Father, if this cannot pass away unless I drink it, Your will be done." Again He came and found them sleeping, for their eyes were heavy. And He left them again, and went away and prayed a third time, saying the same thing once more. Then He came to the disciples and said to them, "Are you still sleeping and resting? Behold, the hour is at hand and the Son of Man is being betrayed into the hands of sinners. Get up, let us be going; behold, the one who betrays Me is at hand!"* (Matthew 26:36–46)

⧗   *Do you struggle to "stay alert" in prayer?*

⧗   *Are there any disciplines you could incorporate into your prayer life to become an active participant in prayer rather than a sleepy observer?*

However, unlike Peter, I have never cut off the ear of someone with whom I disagree! As Jesus, James, John, and Peter began to leave the Garden of Gethsemane that historic evening, they were approached by Judas and the Roman Cohort. The hour of Jesus was at hand, and I am sure the three dear friends of Jesus were horrified by what was taking place before their very eyes. I am also certain they were dealing with guilt over their lazy decision to sleep rather than pray. Instead of looking to Jesus for leadership during this intense and emotional experience, Peter reacted emotionally.

> **Simon Peter then, having a sword, drew it and struck the high priest's slave, and cut off his right ear; and the slave's name was Malchus. So Jesus said to Peter, "Put the sword into the sheath; the cup which the Father has given Me, shall I not drink it?" (John 18:10–11)**

Once again, Peter is forced to look into the eyes of Jesus knowing his actions have not honored the One who loved him. I, too, know that same pain. Perhaps you do too.

⧗   *What do you do when you have a regret in life?*

⧗   *Is there a Bible verse that helps you deal with regrets?*

Sadly, we are not yet done viewing the weaknesses of Peter, this young man who was filled to overflowing with potential. In the hours following his refusal to pray rather than sleep, Peter denied the Lord three wretched times. Jesus had warned Peter of this possibility before the Garden of Gethsemane and prior to Peter's violent reaction to the Roman soldier.

> *But Peter said to Him, "Even though all may fall away because of You, I will never fall away." Jesus said to him, "Truly I say to you that this very night, before a rooster crows, you will deny Me three times." Peter said to Him, "Even if I have to die with You, I will not deny You." All the disciples said the same thing too.* (Matthew 26:33–35)

Although Peter's intentions were pure, he sadly lacked willpower. His heart was sincere in its desire to faithfully give allegiance to Christ, but he lacked the inner resolve to follow through on his well-meaning promise. The horrifying betrayal echoes through the ages and causes modern-day disciples to carefully examine their own hearts.

> *Now Peter was sitting outside in the courtyard, and a servant-girl came to him and said, "You too were with Jesus the Galilean." But he denied it before them all, saying, "I do not know what you are talking about." When he had gone out to the gateway, another servant-girl saw him and said to those who were there, "This man was with Jesus of Nazareth." And again he denied it with an oath, "I do not know the man." A little later the bystanders came up and said to Peter, "Surely you too are one of them; for even the way you talk gives you away." Then he began to curse and swear, "I do not know the man!" And immediately a rooster crowed. And Peter remembered the word which Jesus had said, "Before a rooster crows, you will deny Me three times." And he went out and wept bitterly.* (Matthew 26:69–75)

⧗ *What emotions rise up in you as you read the account of Peter's betrayal? Do you see yourself in this passage at all?*

⧗ *What is one weakness that keeps you from being a bold witness for Jesus?*

Peter and His Issues

As we observe Peter's repeated failures in Scripture, it is certain this man whom Jesus chose to build His church upon, dealt with underlying issues of weakness. Perhaps Peter wrestled with his self-esteem and then contended with personality reactions exacerbated by his blunders.

One of the challenges that continuously rears its ugly head in my life is that of comparison. I often battle the enemy of comparison in my attempt to build a life that honors Christ. Perhaps this mistake-plagued disciple clashed with the fragility that comparison ushered in, as well. If we could get into Peter's head during his early years, we might have heard some thoughts like these:

> *I am just not as educated as Matthew.*
> *I am not as sweet and loving as John. He always says the right thing.*
> *Look at Philip. He is such a deep thinker. Why can't I be more like Philip!*
> *And Simon is always so passionate about Jesus. I am only passionate about me!*

Pondering Peter

We will soon discover that Peter transformed dramatically as he matured. Isn't it wonderful to know no one is beyond help? It's never too late for any of us to change. It wasn't too late for Peter and it's not too late for you!

THE MIRROR

Can you summarize what you learned today in just a few lines?

1. _____

2. _____

3. _____

ETERNAL WORDS

According to the foreknowledge of God the Father, by the sanctifying work of the Spirit, to obey Jesus Christ and be sprinkled with His blood: May grace and peace be yours in the fullest measure. (**1 Peter 1:2**)

MY PRAYER FOR TODAY

Dear Jesus, today I give you my issues. I pray You will transform me and empower me. Today is the day I choose to immediately follow You and serve You. I pray for Your strength to overwhelm me and for Your presence to stay with me. In Jesus' name I pray. Amen.

Day 2

What Happened to Peter?

As we study the book of 1 Peter together, we might be inclined to incredulously ask the question, *What in the world happened to Peter?* We will discover in the five sacred chapters of this astounding New Testament book how Peter is no longer filled with self and opinion, but he has become a wise and substantial teacher. While Peter was formerly strangled by his emotions, now he is led by the Holy Spirit.

Two singular events transformed Peter from being impetuous and opinionated to becoming bold and courageous. Firstly, Peter saw the risen Lord with his very own eyes, and he experienced the joy that only the resurrection of Christ offers.

> *Simon Peter went up and drew the net to land, full of large fish, a hundred and fifty-three; and although there were so many, the net was not torn.*
>
> *Jesus said to them, "Come and have breakfast." None of the disciples ventured to question Him, "Who are You?" knowing that it was the Lord. Jesus came and took the bread and gave it to them, and the fish likewise. This is now the third time that Jesus was manifested to the disciples, after He was raised from the dead. (John 21:11–14)*

Not only did Peter gloriously and emphatically see the resurrected Christ, but then Peter was also filled with the power of the Holy Spirit on the day of Pentecost.

> *When the day of Pentecost had come, they were all together in one place. And suddenly there came from heaven a noise like a violent rushing wind, and it filled the whole house where they were sitting. And there appeared to them tongues as of fire distributing themselves, and they rested on each one of them. And they were all filled with the Holy Spirit*

and began to speak with other tongues, as the Spirit was giving them utterance.

But Peter, taking his stand with the eleven, raised his voice and declared to them: "Men of Judea and all you who live in Jerusalem, let this be known to you and give heed to my words. For these men are not drunk, as you suppose, for it is only the third hour of the day; but this is what was spoken of through the prophet Joel:

'AND IT SHALL BE IN THE LAST DAYS,' **God says,**
'THAT I WILL POUR FORTH OF MY SPIRIT ON ALL MANKIND;
AND YOUR SONS AND YOUR DAUGHTERS SHALL PROPHESY,
AND YOUR YOUNG MEN SHALL SEE VISIONS,
AND YOUR OLD MEN SHALL DREAM DREAMS.'" **(Acts 2:1–4, 14–17)**

These two life-changing events, experiencing the Risen Lord and being filled with the power of the Holy Spirit, are guaranteed to change anyone! So, what about you?

⌛ *How did receiving Jesus as your Lord and Savior change your life? Be specific.*

⌛ *What does it mean to you to be "filled with the Holy Spirit"?*

Prepare to Be Transformed

Peter, who was formerly known as the failure, the attacker, and the denier, began to walk in authority as the rock upon which Jesus would build His church. Peter was the first head of the New Testament church, and his reputation grew into one of strength and steadfastness. His voice of wisdom is now heard nearly two thousand years after he lived on earth. Peter's life is a resounding miracle. When Jesus found him, he was a stinky, ordinary fisherman who miraculously became a first-century evangelist and exemplary leader. Peter, who was dismally known as a denier, became a powerful proclaimer.

My friend, are you prepared to be transformed just as Peter was? Are you ready to live a life of godly impact?

⧗ *What does God need to change in you?*

⧗ *What weaknesses have held you back from living in your God-ordained destiny?*

When

The book of 1 Peter was written from Rome in about 67 AD—this is also when the great persecution under the Roman Emperor Nero began. The madman, Nero, is considered to be one of the greatest criminals in history. He particularly targeted the men and women who chose to be known as "Christians."

Under Nero's rule, Christians were hunted down, killed, and burned at the stake. Members of "The Way" were fed to starving, ravenous lions and were put to death in the most horrific manner for the amusement of Roman citizens.

> In their very deaths they were made the subjects of sport: for they were covered with the hides of wild beasts, and worried to death by dogs, or nailed to crosses, or set fire to, and when the day waned, burned to serve for the evening lights. Nero offered his own garden players for the spectacle, and exhibited a Circensian game, indiscriminately mingling with the common people in the dress of a charioteer, or else standing in his chariot. For this cause a feeling of

compassion arose towards the sufferers, though guilty and deserving of exemplary capital punishment, because they seemed not to be cut off for the public good, but were victims of the ferocity of one man.[3]

⧗ *Have you sacrificed anything meaningful for the cause of Christ? If so, share about it here. If not, write a prayer asking God to help you be willing to sacrifice for Him.*

Why

Peter was compelled by the Holy Spirit to write the book of 1 Peter as a means of encouraging believers who were suffering and being persecuted.

When a New Testament Christian made a public profession of faith and was baptized according to the instruction of Scripture, a victorious parade ensued. Members of the early church marched triumphantly through the streets of Rome—some with blazing torches and others holding majestic palm branches. As they tramped through the streets with the joy only known to a Christian, they sang out the exultant songs of faith for all to hear. The defining declaration of a believer just before he or she descended into the cleansing waters of forgiveness was this, "I renounce the devil and all of his ways!" The jubilant cry of his or her brothers and sisters in Christ rang out into the darkness of the culture.

However, as the newly baptized and thoroughly soaked believers prepared to return home in the darkness of night, Romans soldiers often expectantly waited. The Christians were either immediately killed, or worse still, the cruel soldiers slaughtered the children while the parents were forced to watch. Then, the parents were thrown into the abysmal blackness of a Roman prison cell.

Peter is writing to the people of the early church who sacrificed *everything* for the cause of Jesus Christ. He is also writing to you and to me who are called to make our own sacrifices.

I pray we never face the same type of persecution these precious believers faced. I pray we will never be confronted with martyrdom and torture.

However, we all are accosted by trials, disappointments, misunderstandings, and ridicule. We need to be prepared to march through our culture with our torch of faith burning brightly. We should not be surprised when the world mocks our profession of faith or when the culture condemns our joy. The book of 1 Peter offers insight and wisdom for a church dealing with persecution. Certainly, as twenty-first-century believers, we also require the strength the Holy Spirit presents on these timeless pages.

⌛   *Have you ever suffered from persecution due to a stand you took?*

⌛   *How do you believe a Christian should prepare for persecution?*

A Microphone

Peter stepped from time into eternity about three years after writing this incomparable book of Scripture. Tradition recounts the fact that Peter was crucified upside down because he felt unworthy to die in the same manner as his Savior. The Roman government, of course, was only too happy to comply.

Peter's intent was to write his letter to the early church who were bullied by the culture, persecuted by politicians, and minimalized by a madman. What Peter was unable to fully comprehend was he was writing to all generations of Christians in all the centuries yet to come. The Holy Spirit used the uneducated, passionate fisherman as a microphone to speak to the church of the twenty-first century. The book of 1 Peter was divinely designed and sacredly created to bring hope to a people who know heaven might be only one breath away.

What a timeless way to live . . . just one breath away from seeing Jesus, face to face!

THE MIRROR

When you think of stepping from time into eternity, are you frightened or excited? Explain your answer.

ETERNAL WORDS

According to the foreknowledge of God the Father, by the sanctifying work of the Spirit, to obey Jesus Christ and be sprinkled with His blood: May grace and peace be yours in the fullest measure. (1 Peter 1:2)

MY PRAYER FOR TODAY

Dear Jesus, help my unwillingness. I give you my stubborn heart and ask You to make me willing to say a resounding "Yes!" to You, no matter the cost. Give me the courage of Daniel in the lions' den and the three Hebrew boys in the fiery furnace. Use me, Father, to make hell smaller and heaven bigger. In the mighty name of Jesus, I pray. Amen.

Day 3

Who Are You?

Do you remember those days in elementary school when you wondered if anyone would choose you to be on the kickball team? High school prom gave me that kind of angst. I waited for someone—anyone—to choose me as their date. In college, I watched other girls enjoying numerous dates with handsome boys while I languished in the dorm room most Friday nights. Would anyone ever choose me?

When someone chooses you, it attaches value to who you are as a person. Whether you are eight years old, eighteen years old or seventy-eight years old, a woman aches to know she is worthy to be chosen. Let me assure you, my friend, you are chosen.

> *Peter, an apostle of Jesus Christ,*
> *To those who reside as aliens, scattered throughout Pontus, Galatia,*
> *Cappadocia, Asia, and Bithynia, who are chosen.* **(1 Peter 1:1)**

Peter is a man on a mission from God. He identifies himself as an apostle or a delegate sent forth with specific orders. In ancient days, when writing a letter, the writer identified the authorship at the onset of the communication, whereas today, the writer makes himself or herself known at the end. In the passage above, not only does Peter inform the reader who he is but instantly he reminds the reader who he or she is as well.

You are chosen. You were "picked out" or hand-selected by God to be part of His enormous and loving family that extends through the ages of time. So, let's reflect.

⧗ *What does it mean to you that you have been chosen?*

A Catalog

After experiencing the liveliness and perpetual motion of three rambunctious boys, we were then blessed with two delightful, peaceful little girls. I wept each time I gave birth to a child because my heart felt so overwhelmed with gratitude that God would entrust me as the guardian of the next generation. I must say, however, when the doctor's voice exclaimed, "It's a girl!" with the birth of baby number four, I was so excited I nearly jumped off the birthing table.

With mascara running down my weary cheeks, I looked into the deep blue eyes of my dearly loved husband and declared, "Now I get to go down the doll aisle at Christmastime."

I couldn't wait to bequeath my childhood canopy bed to a little girl and then read *Anne of Green Gables* and *Little House in the Big Woods* together. Then, nearly four years after the birth of Carolyn Joy, we were given a surprise baby girl, whom we named after both of our mothers, Joni Rebecca. We completed our family with three older brothers and two little girls.

Every night when I tucked my little miracles dressed in pink-flowered nighties into their white-and-pink canopy bed, I reminded them. "If Jesus gave me a catalog filled with the faces of all the little girls from around the world and said to me, 'You can choose whichever ones you want,' I would look at all of the pages until I found your faces. I would choose you. You are the little girls I have always wanted!"

Did you know God, the Father, feels the exact same way about you? He chose you for His very own. You were specifically chosen by the Lord to bask in His love and to splash in His goodness. His work on planet earth will not be complete without your enthusiasm and potential.

⧗   *How would you describe your childhood in three words?*

1. _____

2. _____

3. _____

⧗   *As a child, did you know you were loved unconditionally by your parents?*

An Identity Crisis

When you realize you were chosen by the Creator of the Universe, you will begin to comprehend there's no need for you to have a crisis of identity. You were designed in His image and created for His marvelous plans.

> *For You formed my inward parts;*
> *You wove me in my mother's womb.*
> *I will give thanks to You, for I am fearfully and wonderfully made;*
> *Wonderful are Your works,*
> *And my soul knows it very well.* **(Psalm 139:13–14)**

You are a woman of timeless significance because the One who made you values you. The One who created you determines your worth as a woman. If you struggle with self-esteem or comparison issues, remind yourself of this eternal truth every day, *I am chosen by God.*

The Greek word for "chosen" is *eklektos* and is a compound of the words *ek* and *lego.* The prefix *ek* means "out" and the root of the word *lego* means "I say." When these two words are joined and form a compound word, the newly built word literally means "Out. I say."[4]

God loves you so much, dear one. He has called you out of eternal darkness and invited you to a timeless life of significance in His kingdom of righteousness, peace, and joy. Your life matters to Him—you were personally selected by Him. Your acceptance or denial of this truth impacts where you focus your thoughts.

⏳ *Do you compare yourself with others?*

⏳ *When you compare yourself, what are some of the emotions you feel?*

Who Me? Yes You!

This word *eklektos* can also be translated as "choice, select, i.e. the best of its kind or class, excellence preeminent . . .; by implication, favorite."[5]

One way you were especially chosen by God is for service. At once, it holds great encouragement and serious responsibility. You are His favorite daughter and He deems everything about you excellent or the best of its kind. Again, remind yourself of this timeless truth every day: *I am chosen because God values me. I am chosen because God made me. I must agree with God's assessment of my value and worth. I must not argue with God.*

The word *eklectos* expresses anything *especially* chosen because it is outstanding in its field, such as "choice fruit" or "choice meat." It also implies being chosen for a great exploit in the manner that troops are handpicked for battle or a painting set aside for its stunning beauty.

You have been chosen by the Lord and He will utilize your unique abilities, your divine talents, and your sanctified personality for His eternal purposes. You are chosen to:

- Love difficult people
- Bring light to dark places
- Inject hope into hopeless situations
- Choose joy in the midst of discouragement
- Live righteously in the midst of compromise
- Pray for heaven to invade earth
- Make hell smaller and heaven bigger
- Encourage the discouraged
- Pray for the sick
- Be a friend to the lonely

⧗ *Read the above list again and ask the Holy Spirit to speak to you concerning your specific assignment in life. Now, add two or three more items to your choice list.*

1. _____

2. _____

3. _____

In Every Generation

God hand selects, in every generation, men and women who are bold enough and audacious enough to serve Him wholeheartedly. God only requires your yes for service in His household.

> **But you are a chosen generation. (1 Peter 2:9 NKJV)**

God wisely calculated who He needed to serve Him during the early days of the twenty-first century and you were chosen by Him. You are the one elected to:

- Stand up against a fallen culture
- Love the unlovable
- Speak His words
- Give your whole heart in His service
- Compose the worship songs for this generation
- Bring peace to conflict
- Be an encouragement on social media

⧗ *Can you think of any other assignments specific to this generation? List them below:*

1. _____
2. _____
3. _____

You Don't Belong

As one expressly chosen, you no longer belong to this fallen world. Remember the meaning of *eklektos*, "Out. I say." Another point to consider is the One who has set you apart is also the One who determines your homeland.

> **Peter, an apostle of Jesus Christ,**
> **To those who reside as aliens ... (1 Peter 1:1)**

You are merely passing through this earthly kingdom and, as such, your patriotism lies on the foreign soil of eternity's shore. America is not your "Father-land," and neither is earth. You were sent from your homeland to reside with the natives on this planet. This land, as beautiful and breathtaking as it is, should not pull on your heartstrings—eternity is where your true loyalty lies. Your national anthem is not "The Star-Spangled Banner" or "God Save the King," but will forever be "Amazing Grace."

As an alien, your allegiance is not to an earthly flag or to a temporary government, but you should only pledge allegiance to the King of all Kings and the Lord of all Lords.

The things of this life should have no secure hold on your heart or on your mind. Money, possessions, education, travel, sports, homes, and creature comforts were never meant to be your priority. You can enjoy the things of this world while you are traveling through but do not allow temporary, tangible treasures to control you. You can hold them but do not allow them to hold you.

You are a tourist, my friend. Take pictures and enjoy the view but always remind yourself that you are going home someday soon. As a visitor, you speak a different language than the ones normal to an earthly existence. The native tongue of your far-away land is praise and worship. Although the people who live on earth will not always understand your language, speak it loudly and passionately.

As foreigners, we also celebrate different holidays, embrace vastly different goals, are drawn to eternal desires rather than temporary ones, and even eat different food. We eat the "Bread of Life" and feast on His very presence.

It is vital to change the world while we are here rather than allowing the world to change us. We need to consider how we influence others.

⧗ *How can you change the world while you are here? Be specific.*

⧗ *Can you think of other ways Christians are different from the world other than the ones stated above?*

I Love It

The Greek word for "alien" is *paroikos*, which means "someone who was in a strange land and whose thoughts always turned to home." This tender word implies the stranger has the internal assurance that home is near.[6] I have heard that *paroikos*, in its adjective form, can longingly be translated as "homesick."

Doesn't that definition make your heart just ache for heaven? We are identified as the ones who are chosen and homesick.

THE MIRROR

Now that you know how Peter and the Holy Spirit identify you, how will it make a difference in the way you live? Be specific.

ETERNAL WORDS

According to the foreknowledge of God the Father, by the sanctifying work of the Spirit, to obey Jesus Christ and be sprinkled with His blood: May grace and peace be yours in the fullest measure. (1 Peter 1:2)

MY PRAYER FOR TODAY

Jesus, I belong to You and I will never belong to anyone else. Thank You for choosing me and for placing value on my life. Thank You for setting me apart for specific service in Your eternal Kingdom. Lord, I am homesick for You and for my true home. Thank You that someday we will be together forever. In Jesus' name I pray. Amen.

Day 4

Who Is God?

I love digging for gold in the never-changing, always applicable, ever hopeful Word of God. One of the delights of this treasured practice is finding verses in the New Testament in which all three members of the Trinity are mentioned. First Peter 1:2 is such a verse:

According to the foreknowledge of God the Father, by the sanctifying work of the Spirit, to obey Jesus Christ and be sprinkled with His blood: May grace and peace be yours in the fullest measure.

All three members of the Trinity are at work in your life—the Father, the Son, and the Holy Spirit.

Three In One

The Father knows all about you because He is the One who created you and is intimately acquainted with all your ways. Just like a concerned and loving parent, the Father knows when you lay your head down at night, what concerns you, and what is the very best for you. Your heavenly Father cares deeply about your future and how others treat you. After all, you have been on His mind since the beginning of time.

Your eyes have seen my unformed substance;
And in Your book were all written
The days that were ordained for me,
When as yet there was not one of them. (Psalm 139:16)

Peter reminds the early church and therefore those in every generation to come, it is the Holy Spirit who sanctifies believers in Christ. The Holy Spirit teaches how to live a holy life that honors God and His Word. When you are struggling with sin or wrestling with a decision, the little voice you hear is not your conscience, it is the Holy Spirit at work in your life. The Holy Spirit calls you to imitate Christ and then He gives you the power to do it. The Holy Spirit, who is your Comforter and Teacher, gives you the power to be a joyful, peaceful, and hopeful Christian.

> *Now may the God of hope fill you with all joy and peace in believing, so that you will abound in hope by the power of the Holy Spirit.* (Romans 15:13)

The third member of the Trinity is Jesus Christ and among His assignments are to forgive, cleanse with His blood, heal, and open the way to heaven. Jesus also enables you to live a victorious and abundant life.

> *But thanks be to God, who gives us the victory through our Lord Jesus Christ.* (1 Corinthians 15:57)

Every victory you win in your daily walk is all because of Jesus. He leads you in triumph and He wants you to prevail in the battles you face daily, hourly, and even minute by minute. It is Jesus who enables you to win:

- the victory over sin
- the victory of forgiveness both in your own life and the forgiveness you extend to others
- the victory of healing
- the victory of living a righteous, joyful, and peaceful life
- the victory over death

Jesus won the victory on the cross of Calvary and now He shares that victory with us. Jesus also has the joyful assignment of ensuring our lives are not maneuvered by the enemy but are determined by Christ's presence in our hearts.

> *The thief comes only to steal and kill and destroy; I came that they may have life, and have it abundantly.* (John 10:10)

The Father knows you, the Holy Spirit consecrates you, and Jesus cleanses you. There could be no better news than this for a suffering, scattered church. We must know who God is in our deepest moments of pain. When life is at its worst, the only shelter able to keep us safe is the haven of our relationship with God. The timeless knowledge that He cares will prove enough to carry us through the storms of life.

> *What comes into our minds when we think about God*
> *is the most important thing about us.*

> —A. W. Tozer

Now that you have read the above paragraphs, in your own words describe what each member of the Trinity does in your personal life:

1. *The Father*

2. *The Son*

3. *The Holy Spirit*

Your Assignment

Peter is intent about communicating what the members of the Trinity offer to Christians but he also explains what our response should be to their involvement in our lives. Our job description is to obey—that's it. We get to obey our Father who knows us, Jesus who has forgiven us, and the Holy Spirit who helps us when we are weak.

One of the problematic matters of our modern culture and of the twenty-first-century church is we no longer honor the Word of God as did former generations. The truth of the Bible is debated, its eternal principles are mocked, and its substance is ignored. My friend, settle this issue in your life immediately.

The Holy Bible is the divinely inspired, authoritative, and timeless Word of God. On the sacred pages of Scripture are written God's mind and heart toward His children. How wonderful to know God loves us enough to communicate with us. He didn't leave us alone in this fallen world and say, "Do it on your own." God has given us the Bible to direct our lives, to help determine difficult decisions, and to comfort us when we are broken.

If God says no concerning a particular behavior or desire, then the answer is simply no. What God deems as sin will never change through the ages of humanity. God's no is not a soft no—it is a definitive "absolutely not." When God says no to a particular moral habit, it must never be interpreted as:

- Maybe
- Maybe not
- In some cases

- For everyone else but not for me
- Not yet
- Perhaps at some conceivable time in the future

Whenever God says no to sin, He is saying an enthusiastic yes to living an abundant life filled with grace, joy, and peace. Who wouldn't want that?

When a person invites Jesus Christ to live in their heart and asks Him to forgive their sin, a benefit follows. They receive an invitation to participate in the joy of obedience. You now "get" to live your one glorious life according to the timeless principles found in the Word of God.

My friend, do not whine about God's plan for your life or question if God really knows what He is doing. I can assure you there is certainly no need to worry if the Holy Spirit will give you enough power for what is expected of you. Focus on the delightful fact that you get to obey.

You get to bless difficult people and now you are a cheerful and even extravagant giver. You are invited to cooperate with the Father and allow others to feast on His character in your life. You are summoned by the One who knows you best and loves you the most. Refuse a life of worry and stress; instead, bask in trust and therefore peace. You are beckoned by the powerful Holy Spirit to say no to sin and a triumphant yes to God and all His ways.

⧗   *Is there an area of sin you struggle with? If so, what?*

⧗   *Write out a prayer asking the Holy Spirit to help you say no to sin and yes to God:*

An Extravagant Gift

When you respond to God's invitation of obedience, extraordinary blessing will accompany you all the days of your life. This extravagant and valuable gift is now yours:

May grace and peace be yours in the fullest measure. **(1 Peter 1:2b)**

The world endeavors to ridiculously convince Christians that obedience to the Bible is legalism. Culture attempts to persuade us that the Bible is an old, outdated book. However, we know the Word of God is living and abiding. There is nothing "dead" about the Bible!

For you have been born again not of seed which is perishable but imperishable, that is, through the living and enduring word of God. **(1 Peter 1:23)**

We know now that we are foreigners, just passing through this earthly life. As such, we gladly choose to embrace a different code of ethics than the one the world adheres to. Simply out of unashamed love, we are thrilled to obey our good, good Father.

If you love Me, you will keep My commandments. **(John 14:15)**

Because of obedience, your gift is *"grace and peace in the fullest measure."* Grace in this context comes from the Greek word *charis* and is defined as "that which affords joy, pleasure, delight, sweetness, charm, loveliness."[7] What a magnificent gift *charis* is for obeying the life-giving Word of God.

If we falsely believe the only way to live a delightful life is to obtain every creature comfort our little heart desires, we become disillusioned. We may erroneously assume the most direct route to loveliness is a designer wardrobe, perfectly styled hair, and loads of mascara. Our culture has ardently tried to convince us that pleasure is found in a box of chocolates, a vacation in Hawaii, or by living in our dream home. But as believers in the God of creation we can know—beyond a shadow of doubt—joy, pleasure, delight, sweetness, and loveliness are our advantage when we obey.

The second gift obedience guarantees is the blessing of peace. We live in a world desperate for peace, but it doesn't know where to find it. Governments have spent millions of dollars on weapons, negotiations, and ambassadors, yet organizations are still unable to ensure peace. Christians, however, are assured of the priceless gift of peace when we make obedience to the Lord a priority above all else.

My friend, you are no longer a walking Civil War. As a follower of Jesus Christ, you now possess an inner calm that permeates your very life.

The Greek word for peace is *eirene* and its meanings are vast and pervasive. They include:

- Tranquility in the soul unaffected by outward circumstances or pressures
- The rule of order in place of chaos
- Exemption from rage and the havoc of war
- Security, safety, and prosperity
- Wholeness, completeness

When you embrace the *eirene* delivered to your heart through obedience, you will then conduct yourself peacefully even during circumstances that normally would be traumatic or devastating. The Holy Spirit will release an authoritative peace in the deepest part of your soul when you choose to obey the Bible. You will be given the gift of *eirene* to stabilize you when your life has fallen apart. You will no longer collapse in emotional pain or give in to the chaos around, but you will grab *eirene* by the hand and march joyfully forward with *charis*.

THE MIRROR

⌛ *Why do you think the Bible offers a gift as the result of obedience?*

⌛ *Is there any scriptural way to obtain grace and peace other than obedience? This question might take some thought, but let me give you a clue: Yes. There is. Now, search scripture to discover it!*

ETERNAL WORDS

According to the foreknowledge of God the Father, by the sanctifying work of the Spirit, to obey Jesus Christ and be sprinkled with His blood: May grace and peace be yours in the fullest measure. **(1 Peter 1:2)**

MY PRAYER FOR TODAY

Dear Jesus, I have learned so much today about what you have done for me. Father, thank You for knowing me. Jesus, thank You for forgiving me. Holy Spirit, thank You for giving me the power to obey the Word of God. Thank You, dear Lord, for the gifts of joy and peace. I declare today that I will obey You! In Jesus' name I pray. Amen.

Day 5

Will You Sing?

I remember the first time I saw the movie, *Mary Poppins*, as a little girl. My heart sang in delight. From that instant on, musicals filled my soul with melody and elation. But *Mary Poppins* was only the beginning of my love affair with stories that broke out into song.

I can quote *The Sound of Music* script word for glorious word. The soundtrack playing in my heart often includes the scores to *My Fair Lady*, *Singing in the Rain*, and *White Christmas*. I can sing nearly every lyric to *Brigadoon*, *West Side Story*, *Oklahoma*, and *The Music Man*. Oh, how many times I have wished I could sing like Julie Andrews, Rosemary Clooney, or Barbra Streisand.

Craig and I suffer from the same malaise that plagues most married couples—we are unable to agree on what movie to watch on Friday nights. He inevitably chooses an action flick filled with conflict and adventure. I, on the other hand, always choose a melodious movie. I could watch a musical every day of my life.

At this stage, we have come to a marital compromise and now take turns alternating Friday evenings. However, when it is my turn, my handsome husband automatically exclaims, "Musicals are so unrealistic. I have never seen anyone break into song in the middle of the street. Have you?"

With a sparkle in my eyes, I look up at him in wonder and reply, "Well, we should. Christians should break into unrehearsed song in the middle of every street, in every store, and at every restaurant. Let's do it!"

Craig rolls his eyes at me and settles back to watch my musical choice while I grin with quiet satisfaction. I just enjoy the show and often sing along.

⧖ *Let's have some fun . . . what is your favorite movie?*

⧗   *Has anyone ever made fun of your viewing choice?*

Sing and Obey

Blessed be the God and Father of our Lord Jesus Christ, who according to His great mercy has caused us to be born again to a living hope through the resurrection of Jesus Christ from the dead, to obtain an inheritance which is imperishable and undefiled and will not fade away, reserved in heaven for you. (1 **Peter 1:3–4**)

After Peter details our job description and instructs us to immediately and fully obey the Lord, he then describes how to follow through. Perhaps Peter had a smile on his rugged face as he penned the words that echo through the ages and land in our willing hearts. The apostle who taught the first-century church how to live a vibrant life now calls Christ-followers to a lifestyle of worship. Peter inspires bullied and battered believers to break out into a rare melody of praise.

Obedience begins with worship according to the teaching of Peter. The rich life of *charis* and *eirene* are nestled into the resolve of those who thank God for who He is and what He has done. The only way to possess peace during a stormy season is to focus on the Father and not on the winds and waves. When I am dealing with circumstantial monsoons or situational tornadoes, I remind myself to sing in the rain and keep my eyes on the One who has promised never to leave me or forsake me.

As believers in Jesus Christ, we can begin every morning with a song of praise on our lips rather than by moaning, "Oh no. Not another day!" When we receive a difficult phone call, we can break into a chorus. When others are cruel and demanding, we can discipline ourselves to whistle a happy tune.

And finally, when you lay your head on the pillow at night after a long and arduous day, count your blessings instead of sheep and sing yourself to sleep. Worship is an act of obedience.

⌛ *What is your favorite worship song?*

⌛ *Why do you believe Peter calls a believer to a lifestyle of worship?*

A Radical Life

When a man or a woman chooses to serve Christ and His kingdom, there should be a change so radical that the only way to describe it is their life has started all over again. In short, they are born again.

The term *born again* has become so much a part of our Christian-speak we rarely pause to think about its rich meaning. Let's take the time to ponder those two wonderful words.

Born again offers a beautiful metaphor describing our new life as part of the family of God. We have a new Father and a new bloodline. We are now dead to sin and alive to freedom. We are dead to anger and alive to the peace that passes understanding.

There are two distinct and exciting blessings that accompany our new birth in Christ. Our inheritance is a living hope on earth with the joy of heaven thrown in.

⌛ *List three ways being born again has changed your life:*

1. _____
2. _____
3. _____

Living Hope

Hope provides the joyful and constant expectation of the invasion of God's goodness in the life of a believer.

I went to a Christian university where the theme song was "Something Good Is Going to Happen to You," composed by Ralph Carmichael. I've never forgotten the lyrics nor the way one energetic song formed my life-long theology.

Because I know Jesus Christ, I carry the assured hope His goodness will have the final say in all my life situations. His grace is certainly amazing but so is that birthmark of hope accompanying those who believe.

Peter and the Holy Spirit describe the hope of new birth with the extremely unique adjective of *zao*. This word is filled with a sense of activity and enthusiasm. It is not a lethargic word nor is it mundane. The word *zao* is about to change your life.

Zao can be defined in this manner: "Having vital power in itself and exerting the same upon the soul."[8]

This means you have been born again and now are employed in the family business of expressing the living hope that is your birthright. *Zao* hope is powerful as well as productive—the place of its primary influence is upon one's soul.

A crucial part of the value of *zao* hope is understanding and even celebrating its chief target in the soul. The soul is the birthplace of emotions, passions, feelings, and personality. Therefore, if *zao* hope is allowed to make its mark upon your soul, it will change how you feel about the issues of life, and it will renew your passions. Perhaps your passions used to connect to Netflix, food, or shopping, now because of *zao* hope you become passionate about teaching Sunday school, praying for missionaries, or serving up extra portions of kindness to those around you. *Zao* hope will change what comes out of your mouth, how you treat people, and it might even give you a facelift as it changes your very countenance.

After being born again, you no longer belong to self or sin, but you belong to Him, the One you worship with great adoration and praise. Your life is no longer determined by the whims of people, it is guarded and guided by Jesus, the One who delights you with His uncommon hope. Your point of view now exhibits the goodness of God promised to you in every season of life.

It is easy to feel hopeless about family situations, finances, the health of loved ones, or even the state of the world. But remind yourself daily that you are a woman of energetic hope. As you allow enthusiasm to pour out of your mouth in conversations, you will then breathe hope onto others who are in despair.

> *Be strong and let your heart take courage,*
> *All you who hope in the LORD.* (Psalm 31:24)

A Real Place

The second magnificent blessing of being born again is the promise of our inheritance in heaven. We are given *zao* hope when we are alive and we are promised heaven when we die.

I think about heaven often, do you? My heart aches when I hear songs about heaven and the joy that will be mine when I see Jesus face to face. Time on planet earth was never meant to last forever—we truly are just pilgrims passing through this temporary land. Our bodies will wear out someday, but our spirits will live forever with our favorite threesome—the timeless Trinity.

I hope you are not afraid of death but are looking forward to the wonder and majesty of eternal life in heaven. Although unable to wrap our earthly minds around what awaits us on the other side of time, we know it is more glorious than anything we could ever imagine. Perhaps the Bible does not explain heaven in detail because if we knew how fantastically wonderful it is, we would not want to stay on this planet.

I am one of those girls who completely and thoroughly loves life. I love ordinary days and monumental days. I adore the bright sunshine of summer splashing onto my garden and I long for the softly falling snow of winter. I am filled with uncommon joy as I watch my grandchildren chase fireflies or play catch with a baseball in the backyard. I am thrilled to sing the songs of my faith, to prepare family dinners and to hold my husband's hand on long walks through our neighborhood. There have been moments when I dreaded the ending of this life because I love it all so dearly. But the Holy Spirit has assured me that if I love life in the war zone called earth, I will cherish even more my new home in His presence where there is always fullness of joy.

Heaven is a real place. It is not a fairy-tale palace in the sky, but it exists in splendor and in truth. My friend, I can't wait to cross the finish line and see my Savior and Lord. I will also be giddy with excitement to embrace you as you join me in that actual place of wonder and glory. I'd love to know your thoughts.

⌛   *Are you afraid to die? Why or why not?*

⧗ *What Bible character are you most looking forward to seeing in heaven?*

No Matter What

Scientists state that three vital components are required for a human being to survive. Air, water, and food are the trio of necessary ingredients for sustaining life in a human body. I believe for a person to survive emotionally there are also fundamental certainties crucial to one's mental health. Among these central affirmations is protection.

A human being, man or woman, must be assured they are protected from harm, intrusion, and injury.

> *Who are protected by the power of God through faith for a salvation ready to be revealed in the last time.* (1 Peter 1:5)

I always knew my father would do anything necessary to protect our family. When Dad was at home, I never felt afraid of intruders, fire, or conflict. Today, I am married to a wonderful man who has protected my heart and my life for over forty-five years. Not all women have the same assurance, although they deeply desire it.

Children long to be protected from danger, predators, and bullies. Protection is a sustaining desire no matter one's age, geographical location, or socio-economic level. Everyone yearns to feel safe. Families spend thousands of dollars on security systems to ensure their home is protected from outside trauma or invasion by unwanted trespassers.

Remember, God's impenetrable, perpetual, high-powered protection system is now yours. The power of God can protect you when you stand in faith on His promises. The word Peter and the Holy Spirit chose to describe God's protecting capabilities in the above scripture means "garrisoned." The Greek word *phroureo* paints the picture of a military fort with a deep, hidden part that is literally impenetrable. In ancient history, although the city wall could be attacked, *phroureo* made certain the garrison or innermost part of the city would never be reached by enemy forces.

We are garrisoned by God's promises. No matter what enemy may attack, nothing will ever be able to jar our spirit or destroy our faith. We are protected by the One who loves us. Rest in peace, my friend. Daddy is home.

THE MIRROR

This was a big day, wasn't it? Don't feel overwhelmed by it all but choose your "just one thing" and write it down. What one thing from today's reading seems to be the most valuable?

ETERNAL WORDS

According to the foreknowledge of God the Father, by the sanctifying work of the Spirit, to obey Jesus Christ and be sprinkled with His blood: May grace and peace be yours in the fullest measure. (1 Peter 1:2)

MY PRAYER FOR TODAY

Father, there is so much to thank you for today. Thank you for being my Father and for inviting me to become part of Your big family. Thank You for lively hope and for the promise of heaven. I also thank You, Father, for Your protection over my life. Thank You for being at home in my heart. In Jesus' name I pray. Amen.

Week 2

Inexpressible Joy

Day 1

Greatly Rejoice

The confrontational and bold Peter was not a man who would skirt around a difficult issue or ignore it. Peter had already walked on water, cut off a soldier's ear, and brilliantly preached to the leading religious leaders of the day by the time he wrote his letter to the persecuted church. Peter was a "man's man" and yet possessed an inexpressible joy in his soul. His timeless words echo through the ages to a group of people whose world had fallen apart:

> *In this you greatly rejoice, even though now for a little while, if necessary, you have been distressed by various trials, so that the proof of your faith, being more precious than gold which is perishable, even though tested by fire, may be found to result in praise and glory and honor at the revelation of Jesus Christ. (1 Peter 1:6–7)*

Gurus and Philosophers

Peter didn't encourage the early church to greatly weep, nor did he coach them to greatly complain as a result of their trials. Instead, he said to the scattered, broken, bullied church, "It's time for you to sing!"

Most psychologists and many self-help gurus would likely roll their eyes and quickly disagree with Peter's advice. They might term it as ridiculous, insincere, or even evasive. However, you and I must remember that the Bible is enduring, and it is true. I remind myself often that I don't have a better idea than God does and neither do the most brilliant philosophers of our day.

The advice of Peter is triumphant through the centuries and then hits its intended mark in the hearts of us who live during the atrocities of the twenty-first century. You, my friend, are unable to live an abundant life without embracing this absurd, yet healthy, discipline. Greatly rejoicing with a soaring song when there is absolutely no reason in the natural for you to sing is a choice of unmatched power and defiant resolve.

As people of faith, singing a song of irrepressible joy must be our default. We must greatly rejoice when our hearts are broken. We must greatly rejoice when we have been ignored and forgotten. We must greatly rejoice when we feel like throwing in that infamous towel. We must greatly rejoice. We simply must!

From personal experience, I can assure you this dynamic choice to worship the Lord has saved my emotional life more times than I can count. I often sing at the top of my lungs, with my hands raised in the air, while tears course down my cheeks. The determination to sing when one's heart is breaking might be the purest form of worship God has ever heard—and it surely brings untold delight to His compassionate heart.

> *Through Him then, let us continually offer up a sacrifice of praise to God, that is, the fruit of lips that give thanks to His name.* **(Hebrews 13:15)**

⧗   *What is the most challenging situation you have ever gone through?*

⧗   *If you could do that situation over again, what song would you choose to sing?*

No Other Option

The word for "rejoice" Paul and the Holy Spirit have chosen to use in the vitalizing initial sentence of 1 Peter 1:6 is *agalliao* which was never used by secular Greek writers. When this word, *agalliao*, is used in the New Testament, it always describes a deep spiritual joy.

It was the word Mary used in what is known as the Magnificat:

And Mary said:
"My soul exalts the Lord,
And my spirit has rejoiced in God my Savior." (Luke 1:46–47)

Mary, the mother of Jesus, was determined to worship the Lord even though she was unmarried and pregnant. Certainly, she realized what a great honor had been bestowed upon her young life. Yet still, Mary had to face rejection by her culture and the uncertainty of her relationship with Joseph. At this challenging time, Mary chose to *agallio.*

Agalliao was also the response the Philippian jailer demonstrated when he and his entire household chose to believe in God. This man had heard Paul and Silas worshipping in prison when their chains fell off and the prison doors flew open. Because he now knew the Light of the world, the jailer chose to *agallio,* though he realized he might be killed for allowing Paul and Silas out of prison.

> *And he brought them into his house and set food before them, and rejoiced greatly, having believed in God with his whole household. (Acts 16:34)*

Peter heard the authoritative voice of Jesus when Christ gave the greatest sermon in all Christian history. We know this compelling message as "The Sermon on the Mount." In it, Jesus instructed the massive crowd how to respond during times of fierce persecution. Peter, therefore, had learned from Jesus the challenge to *agallio* when the fires of life threaten to consume.

> *Blessed are you when people insult you and persecute you, and falsely say all kinds of evil against you because of Me. Rejoice and be glad, for your reward in heaven is great; for in the same way they persecuted the prophets who were before you. (Matthew 5:11–12)*

This type of rejoicing, or worship, is always incited by a profound spiritual joy. When you know Christ and His power, there is no other option than to *agallio* in the very face of tragedy and persecution. When you have embraced a living hope, you must *agallio* no matter your circumstances. The ability to "greatly rejoice" is not produced due to your sunny personality, from your happenings, or by what is visible. It comes from the deep assurance that God loves us and He will write the end of our stories well.

⧗ *Why do you believe choosing to rejoice in a trial is a cornerstone of our faith?*

⧗ *How do you believe we benefit from choosing to agallio in the middle of difficult times?*

Why Rejoice?

If you are struggling with this part of the lesson, I'd like to quickly assure you that choosing to worship the Lord is not choosing to ignore the ferocious pain of your life. When you choose to worship the Lord even though your heart is breaking, you are declaring, "Lord, I don't understand what I am going through, but I choose to worship You. I know You are bigger than my heart pain and You are well able to accomplish what concerns me. I believe You are close to the brokenhearted and so I will sing my song of praise to You."

I'd also like to remind you that no suffering will escape the Lord's notice—that assurance alone enables us to rejoice. We can rejoice because of our *zao* hope and because we are born again. We can worship because we are forgiven and because the Holy Spirit gives us His own power. We can sing because heaven is real, and because the Father has known us since the beginning of time. We can rejoice because God's power is timeless.

⧗ *Is there someone in your life going through a trial today?*

⧖   *How could you encourage this person?*

A Faith Issue

I'm about to surprise you. I have decided to become confrontational like Peter was in order to tackle the issue of the defiant, yet healthy choice, to rejoice when your heart is breaking and your circumstances are ferocious. I promise you that this out-of-character behavior will only last for a paragraph or two.

Let's pause for a moment from our study of 1 Peter and read what James, the half-brother of Jesus, wrote on this very topic:

> **Consider it all joy, my brethren, when you encounter various trials, knowing that the testing of your faith produces endurance. (James 1:2–3)**

James reminded the church that the resolve to rejoice in a trial is a faith issue. Like a deer caught in the headlights of pain, when we determine whether to run away, rear up in anger, or to sing, our faith is being tested. This is when I will choose to sing the most resolutely. Will you?

My trust in God is the most substantial aspect of my life. Whatever I'm going through, I have decided not to react emotionally, but will instead respond in faith. I will sing when I despise my circumstances and when my heart is reeling. I will choose to count it all joy because I am a woman with faith in an unseen God. Rejoicing while in a trial is not only the healthiest response of all but it is certainly the most powerful and God-honoring.

Biblically, Peter chimes in and agrees with his ally, James, that rejoicing is indeed a faith issue.

> **In this you greatly rejoice, even though now for a little while, if necessary, you have been distressed by various trials, so that the proof of your faith, being more precious than gold which is perishable, even though tested by fire, may be found to result in praise and glory and honor at the revelation of Jesus Christ. (1 Peter 1:6–7)**

At the time of Peter's writing, gold was considered the most precious commodity known to mankind. An active and living faith is more valuable and superior to gold in worth. Gold is temporary and its value is based on the perception of man. Your faith, however, can never be destroyed and its value is eternal and enduring—it is timeless.

The faith of a Christian who decides to rejoice in a trial grows stronger and more durable than it was before. The faith of a woman who chooses to sing through her sorrow is more valuable than the most priceless commodity known to mankind.

When gold is placed in fire, all the impurities rise to the top and then are skimmed off by the goldsmith. The goldsmith ascertains that the gold has been purified when he can see his reflection in the fine metal. So it is with our faith. When our faith is under fire, every one of our inconsistencies will rise to the top and be seen by those around us. The fires of life reveal our anger issues, our tendency to worry, and our bent toward gossip. A critical spirit, negativity, and the inclination to whine will glaringly reveal themselves in the hot, searing fire of the uncontrollable. God, our perfect Goldsmith, skims those useless weaknesses out of our lives and watches until He can see His reflection in our hearts. We are left with our pure-gold faith, which is lovely, brilliant, and eternally valuable.

⧖ *Write out your definition of the word faith.*

⧖ *Now write out your definition of the word worship.*

At the end of your life, the gold you have accumulated will matter not at all but your faith will. I wonder if God has a trophy case in heaven. Have you ever wondered that? If He does, all the trophies in that impressive case are not for men and women of wealth but for men and women of faith.

THE MIRROR

What were the three main takeaways from this lesson for you personally?

1. _____

2. _____

3. _____

ETERNAL WORDS

In this you greatly rejoice, even though now for a little while, if necessary, you have been distressed by various trials, so that the proof of your faith, being more precious than gold which is perishable, even though tested by fire, may be found to result in praise and glory and honor at the revelation of Jesus Christ. (1 Peter 1:6–7)

MY PRAYER FOR TODAY

Dear Jesus, I long to be a pure-gold Christian. When my faith is in the fire, I deeply desire for worship to come immediately out of my mouth and my heart. I say to You today, dear Father, that the reason I live is to worship You. In Jesus' name I pray. Amen.

Day 2

An Unspoken Blessing

Just imagine it. Peter had seen Jesus, face to face. Peter had gone on long walks down dusty roads with the Man from Galilee and Heaven. Peter had talked with Him about religion, healing, and what eternity would be like. Peter had roasted fish over an open fire with Jesus and might have heard His soft snores while His head lay upon a rock or a mound of grass. Peter had seen water turned into wine with his very own eyes. And knowing Peter like we now do he might have thrown the multiplied loaves like footballs to the back of the massive crowd. Peter had laughed with Jesus, wept with Him, and been encouraged by Him. Peter had also been corrected by Him.

The ears of Peter had heard Jesus proclaim,

> *Because you have seen Me, have you believed? Blessed are they who did not see, and yet believed.* **(John 20:29)**

I wonder if Peter pondered this phrase spoken by the Man who had bid him leave his fishing industry. Regardless, Peter likely understood the unspoken blessing over those who believed Jesus was the Christ, and yet had not seen Him.

Peter, who had viewed the empty tomb, wrote the following scripture to generations who did not have the same in-person opportunity he had. Peter is writing to you and to me.

One Man

> *And though you have not seen Him, you love Him, and though you do not see Him now, but believe in Him, you greatly rejoice with joy inexpressible and full of glory.* **(1 Peter 1:8)**

Christianity is not some abstract idea nor is it based upon a kind, fictional character. Christianity is built upon one Man—Jesus the crucified Christ. You and I do not see Jesus now but someday we will. For now, until we are called into His manifest presence, we are invited to live a life of faith, hope, and joy. We are summoned to worship in moments of great pain, and we are expected to live all our days with an inexpressible and glorious inner joy. This is the blueprint for Christian living at its finest.

When a believer in Christ is facing a dilemma and is unable to ascertain what to say, where to go, or what to do, he or she should always immediately turn to the sacred pages of Scripture. It is there we can know the will of God. On the timeless and magnificent pages of the Bible, you will discover God's perfect will for your life. Here are some examples:

- rejoice in the fire
- embrace *zao* hope
- *agallio* when your heart is broken
- develop a strong and enduring faith
- know you are protected
- enjoy *charis* and *eirene*

⌛ *Can you think of other components, according to Scripture, that are God's perfect and amazing will for your life? List five of them here:*

1. _____
2. _____
3. _____
4. _____
5. _____

A lifestyle of faith makes absolutely no sense to the world, and honestly, it makes little sense even to me at times. But I don't live my life by what makes sense. I enthusiastically live my life by what the Word of God presents. I remind myself often that I am an alien, and as such, I was made for another world and a different culture. The kingdom in which I truly live is a kingdom of righteousness, peace, and joy. The world tells me to give up on my faith when I am surrounded by the searing fire that difficult events have kindled. The culture taunts me with the words, *"Your faith isn't working. Faith is just for fools!"* Pop psychology endeavors to convince me that I have a right to complain, but the Word of God bids me to greatly rejoice with joy inexpressible, regardless of what is happening in my life. I am determined to obey the Word. What will you do?

⧗ *What is your definition of the word joy?*

Unspeakable

Choosing to rejoice with joy inexpressible is a discipline forcing me to control my feelings and to resolutely open my mouth and sing. Worship is not motivated by human emotion but it is the result of setting our gaze and hearts toward the One who sits on the Throne. Worship is an activity of human power that revolutionizes our thought life and our emotions. And most endearing of all, worship makes a deposit of inexpressible joy in the soul of the one who is audacious enough to sing in the fire.

Aneklaletos is the Greek word translated as "inexpressible" or "unspeakable." First Peter 1:8 is the singular time this unique word is used in the New Testament. Peter and the Holy Spirit have chosen to use this uncommon word to describe an uncommon response. When joy bubbles up in your soul in the middle of a storm, there are no words that can masterfully narrate what has happened. The Father has chosen to deliver a joy profoundly deep and richly apparent—yet no words adequately express this brand of joy. It is not natural, but comes from a supernatural place—it is birthed in the choir of affliction.

Peter describes the joy that is ours when we choose to worship during sorrow in yet another unparalleled fashion. He pronounces this one-of-a-kind joy as "full of glory." The joy we are given when we choose to sing in the wilderness of affliction is a joy infused with heaven's glory. This glory does not come from a reserve on earth, but is miraculously given from the portals of paradise. When you choose to rejoice in a trial, you are ushering heaven's glory to earth. Your worship is the conductor that welcomes the atmosphere of heaven to earth.

THE MIRROR

I often think about the scripture reminding me that if I love Jesus, I will keep His commandments. We have read a New Testament commandment today. I hope you will take the time to examine your soul and resolve to worship even when you are in a fire.

ETERNAL WORDS

In this you greatly rejoice, even though now for a little while, if necessary, you have been distressed by various trials, so that the proof of your faith, being more precious than gold which is perishable, even though tested by fire, may be found to result in praise and glory and honor at the revelation of Jesus Christ. (1 Peter 1:6–7)

MY PRAYER FOR TODAY

Lord Jesus, how I love You! How I love to exhibit my love for You through obedience to You. Father, I pray the song of my life will bring glory to Your name and it will deliver heaven to earth. In Jesus' name I pray. Amen.

Day 3

Road Pavers

Who paved the way for you to experience salvation? Perhaps it was your grandparents, your parents, or even a well-loved neighbor. My grandfather led my grandmother to the Lord and in the next generation, my father led my mother into a relationship with Jesus Christ. Some people experience the Lord for the first time in a church setting while others meet Him at home, on the street, or even in the workplace. We all have a salvation story, if we have asked Jesus to forgive our sins and accept us into the family of God.

I met the Lord as a four-year-old during family devotions in our century-old home in the tiny village of Alabama, New York. There was nothing significant about my town and nothing grand about my home—except for the wonderful fact that Jesus lived there with us. My dad, who was a general of the faith, cared deeply that all his children develop a constant and consuming love for his Savior. He didn't just talk about it, but he lived out his passion daily in a visible and powerful manner. I prayed the sinner's prayer with my daddy holding my hand. Some people might believe a four-year-old is too young to make a salvation decision, but I knew what I was doing that night. I have never doubted my salvation. The stirring that began in my pre-school heart lives on today—six decades later. As I reminisce, it makes me wonder about your faith history.

⧗ *What is your salvation story? Write it below and then ask the Lord to open the door for you to share it with someone in the days ahead.*

Amazed by God

Prophets who had lived centuries earlier paved the way for the believers of the first century to know Jesus the Messiah. These prophets were just ordinary men, often insignificant to the hierarchy of their culture. These men were specifically chosen by God to hear His voice and then to speak out His words and His heart.

> *Seeking to know what person or time the Spirit of Christ within them was indicating as He predicted the sufferings of Christ and the glories to follow. It was revealed to them that they were not serving themselves, but you, in these things which now have been announced to you through those who preached the gospel to you by the Holy Spirit sent from heaven—things into which angels long to look.* **(1 Peter 1:11–12)**

These God-ordained prophets lived hundreds of years before the coming of Jesus Christ. They were so amazed by the content of the words they heard from God that they longed for the fulfillment of the Bible to happen in their lifetimes. They prophesied the coming of the Messiah and couldn't wait until He came to save the world and reveal the glory of God.

These men made careful inquiries and searches into the matter of the Messiah. They wondered when and how He would come. They also were conflicted about the suffering He would be forced to endure.

Prophets such as Isaiah, Jeremiah, and Joel spoke what was revealed to them by God. However, in their natural minds they were unable to fully comprehend what they were divinely asked to share with the world. Can you imagine how they felt?

⧖ *Has the Lord ever revealed something to you and then asked you to share it?*

⧗   *Do you believe the gift of prophecy is still given today?*

It's All True

I, too, am amazed as I read Old Testament writings and unexpectedly discover a prophetic word that points to the birth of Jesus Christ as the Messiah. To fully understand the depth of the verses we are studying, let's look at a few instances in the Old Testament where the coming of Jesus Christ was prophesied by mere men.

David prophesied the words of Jesus on the cross as well as the exact treatment He would receive. It is likely David didn't fully comprehend the words God asked him to write over four hundred years before the birth of the Baby in Bethlehem—but he wrote the prophecy out of obedience. As we read David's words from the vantage point of the twenty-first century, we are assured David had heard from God:

> *For the choir director; upon Aijeleth Hashshahar. A Psalm of David.*
> *My God, my God, why have You forsaken me?*
> *Far from my deliverance are the words of my groaning.*
> *For dogs have surrounded me;*
> *A band of evildoers has encompassed me;*
> *They pierced my hands and my feet.*
> *I can count all my bones.*
> *They look, they stare at me;*
> *They divide my garments among them,*
> *And for my clothing they cast lots. (Psalm 22:1, 16–18)*

Although not as well-known as David, the prophet Zechariah, who lived about five hundred years before the birth of Jesus Christ, was also given well-defined details about His coming.

> *Rejoice greatly, O daughter of Zion!*
> *Shout in triumph, O daughter of Jerusalem!*

Behold, your king is coming to you;

He is just and endowed with salvation,

Humble, and mounted on a donkey,

Even on a colt, the foal of a donkey. (Zechariah 9:9)

To the prophet Isaiah, who lived about seven hundred years before the birth of Christ, precise details were revealed concerning the way Christ would die. As you read Isaiah's prophetic words, allow their truth to settle in your heart and remind you that you have a Savior who suffered for your sins, yet triumphantly rose again.

He was despised and forsaken of men,

A man of sorrows and acquainted with grief;

And like one from whom men hide their face

He was despised, and we did not esteem Him.

Surely our griefs He Himself bore,

And our sorrows He carried;

Yet we ourselves esteemed Him stricken,

Smitten of God, and afflicted.

But He was pierced through for our transgressions,

He was crushed for our iniquities;

The chastening for our well-being fell upon Him,

And by His scourging we are healed.

His grave was assigned with wicked men,

Yet He was with a rich man in His death,

Because He had done no violence,

Nor was there any deceit in His mouth. (Isaiah 53:3–5, 9)

Can you imagine someone who lived during the 1300s predicting computers, airplanes, or photography? What a preposterous thought. It's impossible to conceive of a person forecasting cars, electricity, or radio waves five hundred years prior to these marvelous inventions. Four hundred years ago, even educated doctors would never have dreamed that most dreaded diseases would be wiped out by vaccinations. The wonder of machines able to look inside a human body and see its functions would have been unfathomable.

And yet because ordinary men declared, "*Yes, Lord. I will listen to You and communicate Your thoughts to the world I live in,*" we can remain assured that Jesus Christ truly was the Messiah. I am still amazed. Are you?

⧖ *What is the hardest thing the Lord has ever asked you to do? Did you do it? Write about that situation below.*

Because of YOU!

We have the advantage of understanding the prophet's writings more clearly than the prophets themselves. However, after searching and questioning, after asking and inquiring, God revealed to these simple men that they were not serving themselves.

The prophets were serving the generations that would follow. The reason God gave the prophets detailed insight into the suffering of the Messiah was so you and I would believe. Even as I write these words and then re-read them, my heart can barely contain the wonder of God's plan for our benefit.

The prophets continued to write and speak despite severe persecution. Why would an average man do this? They had nothing to gain personally by sharing God's revelation of future events when the prophecies would never be fulfilled in their lifetimes. And why would they continue to prophesy despite the certain torture that faced them? They didn't stop sharing God-given insight because they were thinking about you and me. They knew their words would stir amazement in the hearts of people yet to be born.

My friend, every generation has the responsibility of sharing the words of God with those who will follow them. We must live our lives in such a way that we leave a timeless legacy of the kingdom of God for our descendants. We dare not live for the ease of self or for personal protection. Someone must tell people about Jesus. Will you?

I am able, as a mouthpiece of God in the twenty-first century, to live and speak a legacy of faith, which is far more precious than gold. My children, my children's children, and beyond will know of God's impact on my life. I have been called to share with my children's friends and my neighbors. I am appointed by God to remind the women under my watch that the Bible is true, and heaven is real. My assignment is to gently but powerfully reveal the joy that occurs when a woman is bold enough to worship in a trial.

When a humble man or simple woman hears the voice of God and shares His truth, not only will that person make a difference today, but the good news will echo through the ages of eternity. Just ask David, Isaiah, and Zechariah.

⧖ *List five people you are praying will come to know Jesus as Lord and Savior. After you make your list, commit to pray for them daily. As you pray for each one by name, you can expect the Lord to show you how you can be part of their salvation experience.*

1. _____

2. _____

3. _____

4. _____

5. _____

The Gasp of Heaven

Now that you know about prophets, it's time to talk about angels. Angels are heavenly beings created by God who live in heaven but help carry out His work on earth. Angels long to understand the mysteries of salvation and to see the plan of God unfold through your life. They are keenly interested in observing how your life fits into God's strategic and wonderful blueprint.

> *...in these things which now have been announced to you through those who preached the gospel to you by the Holy Spirit sent from heaven—things into which angels long to look.* (1 Peter 1:12)

The Greek word used for "look" in this particular verse is the word *parakyptō*. This intense word does not imply just a passing glance that shows no interest in a situation but implies the action of stooping down and studying. *Parakyptō* can also mean "to look at with head bowed forward . . . to look carefully into, inspect curiously."[9]

Angels are eternally curious to see what the next episode of your life will present. Why would these heavenly beings, who are ever in the presence of God, possess such a passionate interest in the details of *your* life? The answer to that question is more marvelous than we can dare imagine.

Angels will never experience the endowment of God's character as you and I are able to. Angels will never be washed in the life-changing blood of Jesus Christ as you and I are. Angels will never know the power of the Holy Spirit, or be asked to walk by faith rather than by sight. Nor will they experience the joy of singing in the fires of life. The angels are intently watching our lives as we reveal the gospel story through day by ordinary day.

As you face sorrow and trials, angels are watching you with bated breath and cheering you on to victory in Christ. The angels gasp in amazement as you and I choose to tell the story of Jesus.

THE MIRROR

⧖   *Why do you believe I named this chapter "Road Pavers"? I thought about using the title "Prophets and Angels" but chose this alternate title instead.*

⧖   *If you were the person who named this chapter, what name would you have selected?*

ETERNAL WORDS

In this you greatly rejoice, even though now for a little while, if necessary, you have been distressed by various trials, so that the proof of your faith, being more precious than gold which is perishable, even though tested by fire, may be found to result in praise and glory and honor at the revelation of Jesus Christ. (1 Peter 1:6–7)

MY PRAYER FOR TODAY

Dear Jesus, would you use me to tell the story of Jesus to others? Would you use my life and my voice to speak across the pages of history and impact the generation to come? I pray You would speak to me and give me Your words. Give me boldness to be an enthusiastic witness for You and for Your kingdom. In Jesus' name I pray. Amen.

Day 4

Knowing What It's There For!

One of my favorite theology professors in college joyfully taught, "When you see the word *therefore* in the Bible, you need to figure out what it is there for."

I have never forgotten his wise words. Even to this day, over four decades later, when I see the word *therefore* in the Bible, I peruse the preceding verses to try and discover the reason behind the text. Some people might refer to it as "cause and effect"; however for me, it has always been the *therefore principle* so powerfully taught by the beloved Dr. Jerry Horner.

As we begin the following section, we will challenge ourselves to discover "what the *therefore* is there for."

Lights, Camera, Action!

Therefore, prepare your minds for action (1 **Peter 1:13**).

The reasons believers in Christ should prepare their minds for action are, of course, found in the preceding verse. The *therefore* Peter inserts at this point in his dynamic letter is reflexive to these truths:

- because you now know your life is not about you.
- because you now know you have a responsibility to generations to come.
- because you desire to live with the same intention and impact as did the prophets.
- because you are amazed the heavenly battalion is watching your life intently and is cheering you on.

For those four reasons, and likely many others, Peter now instructs the persecuted, scattered church to "prepare your minds for action." In the ancient Greek, this phrase literally means "gird up the loins of your minds for action."

Peter used "a metaphor derived from the practice of the Orientals, who in order to be unimpeded in their movements were accustomed, when starting a journey or engaging in any work, to bind their long flowing garments closely around their bodies and fastened them with a leather belt."[10]

Can you picture it? Imagine the difficulty of running or working with an enormous amount of extra fabric constricting their movements. But, when the runner or worker pulled the extra material up between the legs and tucked it into their belt, the tunic became more like generous trousers rather than a skirt.

Peter is calling us to follow the same type of action in our thought life. Our human thoughts often race out of control and thus impede our ability to focus on a goal. But we should gather up every worry, question, and critical thought that distracts from the primary purpose of life—telling the story of Jesus. While it is painfully true that some thoughts have no business residing in the mind of a believer, it is our God-given responsibility to ensure those rushing notions leave quickly, and do not take up residence in our gray matter.

It is also vital to address one other aspect of this literal translation that may embarrass some of you. However, we are all adults, so let's not ignore the specific part of our mind that we are instructed to "gird up." Peter is not gentle nor is he genteel in his approach to word usage in this phrase. He uses the metaphor that refers to *the loins of your mind*.

The loins are the specific part of a man's body located between his legs—they are extremely tender and easily injured. It's also in a man's loins where the ability to reproduce takes place. If you are not careful and if you refuse to gird up the loins of your mind, you will be subject to easy injury and unable to reproduce anything healthy. But you can protect yourself when you obey the truth of Scripture.

⧗ *What is one weakness you deal with mentally? Write it below and then ask God to help you "gird up your mind."*

Intense Action

Your mind will encounter intense resistance in your walk with Christ so prepare for it. Gird up those thoughts that possess the potential to cause you to stumble or distract from the correct course in life. Intense action always requires intense preparation.

I have inevitably had to give myself strong and immovable mental boundaries. I remind myself daily that I am not allowed to worry. Every time a worrisome or anxious thought enters my mind, and they often do, I take those unhealthy thoughts captive with the Word of God.

> *Be anxious for nothing, but in everything by prayer and supplication with thanksgiving let your requests be made known to God.* **(Philippians 4:6)**

I resolve not to embrace a critical idea about a person or a group of people. Whenever a negative thought enters my mind concerning a person, I pray a blessing for that one who was made in the image of God and whom He loves dearly.

> *I thank my God in all my remembrance of you, always offering prayer with joy in my every prayer for you all.* **(Philippians 1:3–4)**

When and where does your mind run out of control? Prepare yourself and decide ahead of time what you will do when the unwelcome intrusion begins in your brain. If your challenge is thinking sinful thoughts or pondering inappropriate fantasies, take every thought captive with the power in the Word of God. Apply the Word to your weakness and see what God will do!

> *We are destroying speculations and every lofty thing raised up against the knowledge of God, and we are taking every thought captive to the obedience of Christ.* **(2 Corinthians 10:5)**

⧗ *Can you think of a scripture you can apply to your thought life? Write it below:*

What Do You Do?

I believe this section will help you in a tremendous and life-giving way as you prepare your mind for preemptive action. Read this list of practical reminders concerning a believer's preparation of the tender areas of their minds.

- Take inappropriate thoughts captive immediately with the Word of God.
- Do not linger upon mental sewage or sludge.
- Turn your worries into a prayer.
- Turn criticism into a blessing.
- Stay involved in activities that will renew your mind such as church attendance, Bible study and healthy Christian relationships.
- Listen to Christian music.
- Have a daily quiet time that includes Bible reading and a devotional book.
- Every morning when you wake up, ask the Holy Spirit to help you.

⧗ *Add three more disciplines to the list above that will help you gird up the loins of your mind:*

1. _____

2. _____

3. _____

Are You Using It?

There are many items lying around my house that I own but don't use. I have a huge turkey roaster I only use once a year, a steamer still in its package, and a coffee grinder someone gave me. Just because you own something or because someone gave you a particular gift, doesn't guarantee you will ever use it. However, you were given one potent piece of equipment, something extraordinary of timeless value, that you dare not ignore. This handy tool will enable you to gird up the loins of your mind for whatever comes its way.

But we have the mind of Christ. (1 Corinthians 2:16)

You have the potential to think the very thoughts of Christ! The only way you will ever do this is by reading the Bible and then memorizing God's Word. If you long to truly utilize the mind of Christ, you must ask the Holy Spirit to take control of your mind.

If you are sadly aware your thought life has become a mental train wreck, it is imperative that you retrain your brain. My friend, if you were in a serious accident, you would go to physical therapy and thus retrain your legs or arms to work again in strength and power. Some of us have experienced "mind wrecks." Our minds have collided with our culture, and we need the intensive care unit of the Word of God. Perhaps today is an appropriate time to make an appointment with the Great Physician.

THE MIRROR

⧗   *This is one of those lessons where you might say, "Ouch! That hurt." But the truth is, we all need help with the process of cleaning up our minds. Consider this question. In a practical sense, what does it mean that you have been given the mind of Christ? Be specific:*

ETERNAL WORDS

In this you greatly rejoice, even though now for a little while, if necessary, you have been distressed by various trials, so that the proof of your faith, being more precious than gold which is perishable, even though tested by fire, may be found to result in praise and glory and honor at the revelation of Jesus Christ. (1 Peter 1:6–7)

MY PRAYER FOR TODAY

Dear Jesus, thank You for giving me Your mind. I pray today I will think Your thoughts and dwell on the Word of God. Father, cleanse my brain of all unrighteous thinking and help me to use my mind for the purpose for which it was made. In Jesus' name I pray. Amen.

Day 5

Staying Sober

If you were engaged in a vicious clash of hand-to-hand conflict, you would likely refuse to joke around, act silly, or let some ridiculous fantasy distract you. Your fists would engage in the fierce battle as well as your mind. A large aspect of the challenge to "gird up the loins of your mind" is found in the importance of staying mentally sober. There is a war raging for the most important part of your mind and it is time for you to realize it and take appropriate action.

Everything

How do soldiers act in battle? They are sober and intent on one thought and one thought alone—we must win. They realize their lives and the lives of their comrades are at stake. Every choice they make, every word they say, every thought they think has long-lasting and perhaps fatal consequences.

> *Therefore, prepare your minds for action, keep sober in spirit, fix your hope completely on the grace to be brought to you at the revelation of Jesus Christ. (1 Peter 1:13)*

My friend, everything you do counts! Do not minimize the power of your thought life in your attempt to win the battle for hope and an abundant life. Your thoughts determine the words you speak. You must ensure that only the Word of God comes out of your mouth during the most intense and exasperating moments you face. Your thought life matters to the cause of Jesus Christ, and you must not underestimate the value of girding your mind.

Peter calls battle-weary soldiers from every generation to take their faith seriously and to be sober in spirit. The word translated as *sober in spirit* is the Greek word *nepho*, and it can be translated to mean: *to be sober, to be calm and collected in spirit; to be temperate, dispassionate, circumspect.*

As I read Peter's advice to a church being fed to the lions, burned at the stake, and impaled with poles, I honestly don't know whether I should laugh or cry. How is it possible to remain calm and collected as you hear the death screams of those you love dearly? Does Peter believe it is possible to remain temperate and circumspect while waiting your turn in front of starving lions? Once again, I might be tempted to accuse Peter of offering ridiculous advice.

Peter's instruction would indeed be ridiculous to most—but not to us. We know Jesus Christ and so we can remain sober in spirit. We know where our hope is fixed. Our hope is not tied to an earthly outcome or positive results, but is completely and totally fixed on the grace that is ours because we know Jesus Christ. What are your thoughts?

⧖ *How did you initially feel when you read the definition of the phrase sober in spirit?*

⧖ *Are you able to stay sober in spirit when you are in a trial? If so, why? If not, why not?*

People of Hope

We are the people of hope, and we serve the God of all hope. Hope is the joyful and confident expectation that God will invade our circumstances with His ultimate goodness.

> **Now may the God of hope fill you with all joy and peace in believing, so that you will abound in hope by the power of the Holy Spirit. (Romans 15:13)**

We are so assured of the goodness of God that we defiantly refuse to settle for anything less than hope. When despair knocks on the door of our hearts, we answer with the Word of God and begin to sing the songs of faith that thousands have sung before us. When doubt tries to creep in through the back door, we gird our minds and keep our gaze set on Jesus.

Every believer in every generation has had to settle these issues of faith:

- Will I embrace hope or will I give in to despair?
- Will I worship or will I worry?
- Will I tell the story of Jesus or will I focus on my own pain?
- Will I gird up my mind or will I allow it to run wild?
- Will I stay sober or will I panic?

And not only this, but we also exult in our tribulations, knowing that tribulation brings about perseverance; and perseverance, proven character; and proven character, hope; and hope does not disappoint, because the love of God has been poured out within our hearts through the Holy Spirit who was given to us. **(Romans 5:3–5)**

As I read this corresponding verse written by the apostle Paul in the book of Romans, it reminds me that I was created to sing in the rain and dance in the fires of life. My job description is to refuse panic and to raise my hands in worship even when receiving a devastating doctor's report, when I lose my job, or when someone I love rejects me. According to Scripture, it is the task to which I have been assigned by my Creator.

⧗ *Circle the most important words in the scripture passage from Romans 5:3–5. Take a minute or two to ponder these words.*

⧗ *Why is it impossible for hope to disappoint us?*

The Last Word

I believe God will always have the last word and it will be a good word. I am convinced God is at work behind the scenes writing the end of each of our stories and His endings are amazing.

Hope is not a hazy and unstable desire that all our wishes will come true. And it is certainly not akin to blowing out the blazing candles on a birthday cake. Hope is not wishing on a star nor is it blowing the feather-like seeds off a dead dandelion. Hope, as you know, is the joyful and constant expectation of God's goodness. Hope is knowledge. Hope is factual. Hope takes faith.

Peter calls all of us, in the middle of turmoil, cultural compromise, and heart pain, to firmly set all our hope completely on Jesus. Our hope is not secure in our jobs, our parenting, the economy, politics, or even in our marriage. The only safe place to fix our hope is in Jesus. I have heard it said that life without Christ is a hopeless end but with Christ it is an endless hope. I joyfully concur with that statement. Do you?

THE MIRROR

As I gaze into the mirror this lesson has presented, I realize how often I have failed at staying sober in spirit. I have been known to panic a time or two. Have you? What has proven most helpful in this lesson concerning staying sober in spirit?

ETERNAL WORDS

In this you greatly rejoice, even though now for a little while, if necessary, you have been distressed by various trials, so that the proof of your faith, being more precious than gold which is perishable, even though tested by fire, may be found to result in praise and glory and honor at the revelation of Jesus Christ. (1 Peter 1:6–7)

MY PRAYER FOR TODAY

Dear Jesus, I can't do it without You. I can't stay sober in spirit, and I certainly can't be a hopeful person without Your strength, power, and wisdom. Father, would you do a new work in me today? I deeply long to honor You in every thought I think and in all my emotional responses to life. In Jesus' name I pray. Amen.

Week 3

Imperishable Love

Day 1

Delightfully Different!

As God's children, we are delightfully different and splendidly unique. Some of us have big feet and small noses while others have small feet and big noses. I love to read, listen to music, and watch college basketball while you might enjoy cooking, cleaning, and shopping. Some of God's perfectly created children have soft, blonde curls while others have flaming red hair. Others have a hard time remembering what color their natural hair actually is!

However, the one attribute we should all have in common is that as God's beloved children, we are committed to immediate obedience. The power verse that should be seared into indelible places on our minds and hearts is this:

> *He who has My commandments and keeps them is the one who loves Me.*
> *(John 14:21)*

Obedience is an issue of love just as worship has its foundations in trust. Obedience to Christ is conceived in the petri dish of love.

> *Identify the one area of your life where it is the most difficult for you to be obedient. Then, pause, pray, and ask the Lord to speak with you about that issue as you read this chapter.*

Don't Give In

As obedient children of the Lord, we must make sure we do not give in to our old nature which is controlled by sin. Before we knew Christ, we preferred sin over righteousness, but now that we know Him and love Him, obedience is our highest and most joyful priority.

> *As obedient children, do not be conformed to the former lusts which were yours in your ignorance.* (1 Peter 1:14)

You are born again and assigned a brand-new nature, renewed desires, a transformed personality, and a fresh bent in your everyday choices. We all have former lusts that will continue to plague us, but we can refuse to give in to them, simply out of our deep love for Jesus. I remind myself daily that I love Jesus more than I love spending money, eating too many carbs, feeling frustrated with my husband, or ignoring a world in pain. The only way I will ever escape those dastardly former lusts is by fanning the flames of love for Jesus.

I will stand firm in love and spurn my old nature that was filled with symptoms such as anger, jealousy, comparison, becoming easily offended, talking too much, and being filled with selfish opinions. Peter says those former lusts were ignorant—we weren't very smart when we chose that lustful way of living.

⧖ *What were some of the "lusts" you dealt with before you knew Jesus?*

1. _____
2. _____
3. _____
4. _____
5. _____

⧖ *Do these particular lusts still plague you?*

⧖ *What should you do when these lusts tempt you?*

⧖ *Why do you believe Paul says "the lusts were yours in ignorance"?*

Just Like My Dad

Simply ignoring sin and placing it aside is only part of the battle in the attempt to live an abundant life of honor. We must also replace the sin with a different type of behavior.

> *But like the Holy One who called you, be holy yourselves also in all your behavior.* (1 Peter 1:15)

Obedient children should act just like their Daddy, knowing He is holy. If we desire to obey this verse, we must become acquainted with the nature and character of God. He is the One we are imitating.

In the Old Testament, the word *holy*, when describing the character of God, was the Hebrew word *gadosh*. This word can be interpreted as "apartness, holiness, sacredness, or hallowedness."[11] The call to holiness is an invitation to be separated from sin and then to be pure in thought, speech, and behavior. The Greek word Peter uses to describe the nature of God is *hagios*, which also means to live a life without sin, to be blameless, and to be separated from anything unclean.[12]

When I read the command to live a holy life, I am intimidated. Are you? It seems morally impossible to my human mind to live a life of God-like virtue. However, if I refuse to obey this New Testament command, it suggests I don't love my heavenly Father. That is certainly not true. If I endeavor to obey and then fail, I am right back where I started—living a life of ignorance. There is only One who is Holy and that is God Himself. As I ponder the holiness issue, I presume an ordinary woman would have to be like God to be considered holy. But how in the world will I ever be like Him? Maybe you share my struggle.

Take a deep breath, my friend, because being like God in His holy nature is precisely what Peter is proposing. Every day of our lives, we are to be conformed more and more to the image of the One who made us and who loves us. I do love Him—I love Him with my whole heart—and therefore His holiness should supersede my tendency toward lust and sin. It is imperative I give Him my whole heart so He can give me His heart in return. I am in desperate need of a heart transplant to live a holy life—and He is willing to do the surgery it requires.

The Dreaded List

Holiness can at times be a strictly religious word and it is exhausting to apply it in a practical sense to our everyday lives. The word *holy* conjures up stained glass windows, pipe organs, and endless times of prayer on our knees. We need to change our mindset when we think of this powerful, liberating, and appealing word—holiness.

Nearly every area of your life will be changed for the better when you declare, *Lord, I love you so much that I want to be just like You.*

Holiness is not a drudgery nor is it a boring existence, but it is a lovely invitation to bring the character of God to earth. Serving a holy God was a novel thought in ancient Rome. Roman gods were known as vengeful, angry, bloodthirsty, and promiscuous. Our God is holy, eternally loving, perpetually kind, and always compassionate. As a set-apart people, one of our main goals is to emulate the God we serve. We are not coerced to be like Him, but we are lovingly beckoned to become like Him and to model His heart. Do you hear Him gently calling your name?

⧗   *What are some characteristics of God you would love to obtain in your own life?*

1. _____

2. _____

3. _____

Hard to Be

Over the years of my walk in Christ, it has been effortless to refer to God as holy. I know fully holiness is not merely something He exhibits but it is His very identity. I have loved singing the songs of faith that refer to this component of His character:

Holy, holy, holy! Lord God almighty!
Early in the morning our song shall rise to Thee.[13]

or

You are holy, holy,
Lord there is none like You.[14]

But what is often easy to sing about is more difficult to become. I've experienced many days when it was hard to exhibit holiness, and I have abysmally failed. Holiness is the architectural plan upon which God is building His temple. If I desire to be part of His plan for this generation, then I must, I simply must, respond to His tender invitation. When I try to live a holy life on my own, holiness becomes legalism and a set of unattainable rules. However, when I call on the power of the Holy Spirit, holiness becomes a lifestyle of power and freedom.

One of the challenges in my quest to live a holy life is facing the times I came across as legalistic, preachy, or a goody-two-shoes. The Lord has reminded me that I don't need to preach about the importance of living a holy life, I just need to be the one who demonstrates it. Silence about a holy life does not imply weakness of character but strength of witness.

I am not ashamed to admit I am unable to live a holy life by self-control, self-abasement, or by running to a convent. I need the Holy Spirit to bequeath His absolute strength and unending power. All I need to do is to ask Him for it.

It is a great deal better to live a holy life than to talk about it. Lighthouses do not ring bells and fire cannons to call attention to their shining—they just shine.

—D. L. Moody

As we allow the Holy Spirit to do a strengthening work in our lives, and then quietly yet boldly live a life of godly imitation, we will reveal what a profound difference Jesus can make in one woman's life. We become the living, breathing, walking, talking demonstration of the character of God.

THE MIRROR

⧗ *Is your definition of the word holy now redefined? What did you learn about holiness while reading this chapter?*

ETERNAL WORDS

Knowing that you were not redeemed with perishable things like silver or gold from your futile way of life inherited from your forefathers, but with precious blood, as of a lamb unblemished and spotless, the blood of Christ. **(1 Peter 1:18–19)**

MY PRAYER FOR TODAY

Dear Jesus, I humbly accept your invitation to live a holy and set-apart life. Thank You for choosing me to demonstrate Your amazing character. I do want to be just like You, Dad. In Jesus' name I pray. Amen.

Day 2

The Purpose of Fear

Fear can be a difficult concept to understand on the pages of Scripture. The Bible commands no less than 365 times "not to fear" in some form or another, and yet it also speaks of "the fear of the Lord." It's time for us to take the fear out of fear. Let's get to it!

⧗ *What were you afraid of as a child?*

⧗ *What are you afraid of today?*

Afraid of Dad?

> *If you address as Father the One who impartially judges according to each one's work, conduct yourselves in fear during the time of your stay on earth.* (1 Peter 1:17)

As Christians, we are not to fear God like the slave who lived in abject fear of his master or as the prisoner terrified of a cruel guard. The fear we are to have toward the Father is identified as respect and awe. This level of reverence cannot bear the thought of bringing pain or disappointment to the One whom we love so dearly. We are also fully aware of His unconditional love toward us. We snuggle into His presence when we are lonely. We listen for His voice when we pray. We celebrate the words He has spoken through the Bible. And we must also humbly declare His lordship and His authority in our lives.

And by the fear of the LORD one keeps away from evil (Proverbs 16:6).

As you develop a reverent awe of the Father and a submissive respect of His nature and character, you will then depart from sin and avoid evil on your journey through life.

A person who possesses this healthy fear of the Lord refuses to take His generous grace for granted and is keenly aware of the price paid for salvation and forgiveness. Our privileged status as God's beloved children does not give us the right to do whatever we want—we must stay morally alert in all situations and at all times. We are not spoiled brats, but grateful children with obedient hearts. As the precious children of the Most High God, we no longer live a life of wanton pleasure but choose respectful cooperation.

I long to be perpetually aware of living in His presence rather than focusing on my passing fancies or selfish desires. I remind myself daily that I am serving the Lord with every word I speak, every choice I make, every dollar I spend, and even with every facial expression. Although I live and breathe as a human being on earth, I am still in His presence.

Do not be hasty in word or impulsive in thought to bring up a matter in the presence of God. For God is in heaven and you are on the earth; therefore let your words be few. (Ecclesiastes 5:2)

⏳ *In addition to loving God and obeying Him, Peter invites us to fear the Lord. Why do you believe "fearing the Lord" is an important aspect of our Christian lifestyle?*

Someone

Did you know that someone died for you? Someone left His precious blood at the crime scene of your sin.

Knowing that you were not redeemed with perishable things like silver or gold from your futile way of life inherited from your forefathers, but with precious blood, as of a lamb unblemished and spotless, the blood of Christ. **(1 Peter 1:18–19)**

Slavery was a horrible part of the culture in the days of the early church. Men and women were placed into servitude for the slightest infraction or the smallest weakness. Often, innocent men and women were forced to remain in slavery until someone could afford to buy their freedom back.

In ancient days, only the next of kin or closest family member was allowed to buy back a slave from servanthood. Mere money was never enough to set a slave free. Oftentimes the entirety of someone's life savings, all their valuables and goods, was required to buy a slave his or her freedom. The word *redeemed* in the passage above is the same economic word used to describe the process of buying freedom for a slave.

⧗ *Do you ever feel like a slave?*

⧗ *What causes that feeling in your life?*

My friend, God didn't purchase you with gold from the kingdom of darkness—He deals in a different form of currency. Gold has no eternal value for God, it is mere pavement material in heaven. Before Jesus paid your price, you were in slavery to sin and in bondage to the kingdom of darkness. The wrong owner had possession of you and there was absolutely nothing you could do about it. You couldn't afford the price required to remove the shackles of sin and shame keeping you imprisoned. A family member who could afford the price had to step forward and redeem you or you would have stayed in slavery forever. You had no hope without a next of kin.

Someone did step forward, however, and He bought you back. Your elder brother paid for your redemption with His precious blood. His spilled blood covered your freedom. He exchanged His very life for yours. That Someone is Jesus!

THE MIRROR

⌛   *One of the scriptures I referenced in this chapter was Ecclesiastes 5:2. Go back and read it again. Now, take the time to write it out in your own words below:*

ETERNAL WORDS

Knowing that you were not redeemed with perishable things like silver or gold from your futile way of life inherited from your forefathers, but with precious blood, as of a lamb unblemished and spotless, the blood of Christ. (1 Peter 1:18–19)

MY PRAYER FOR TODAY

Dear Jesus, thank You for redeeming me. Thank You for paying the price for my sins and for buying me back from slavery. Help me to live in a way that honors You all the days of my life. I am not afraid of You, Father, but I do respect and stand in awe of all You have done for me. In Jesus' name I pray. Amen.

Day 3

Jesus Was Always the Plan

One of the greatest challenges in human relationships is discerning how others truly feel about us. As women, we are acutely aware of nonverbal signals, snubs, and the ache of cool treatment by those we would love to have a relationship with. Maybe similar thoughts to the following have crossed your mind.

She didn't even make eye contact with me. Maybe we are not as close as I thought we were.

We have been married for thirty years, but does he still love me? I have gained weight, my wrinkles are so wrinkly, and my hair is thinning and gray. I'll bet he is thinking about his high school girlfriend. I can just tell there is something wrong.

The pastor's wife walked right by me in church this week. She doesn't appreciate everything I do for this church. I guess I am just not part of the "in" crowd.

My friend, you no longer need to wonder how God feels about you. His heart's desire is to spend all of eternity with you. He will never tire of your company.

⧗ *Other than Jesus and potentially your spouse, who has been your best friend throughout the years of your life?*

⌛   *Now, rather than feeling slighted because someone else didn't take initiative, is there someone you should reach out to in friendship this week? Is there a lonely or insecure woman you could encourage or spend time with?*

For the Sake of You

Did you know Jesus was not an afterthought to God's timeless and perfect plan? When Adam and Eve questioned God's Word in the Garden of Eden and listened to the serpent, God didn't throw His holy hands up in the air and despairingly say, *"Oh no! Adam and Eve just blew it. Now what am I going to do?"* Jesus was always the plan.

> **For He was foreknown before the foundation of the world, but has appeared in these last times for the sake of you. (1 Peter 1:20)**

God was fully aware in all of eternity past that you and I would need a Savior and so He sent Jesus *"for the sake of you."* Don't those five achingly beautiful words just make you weep? Jesus came *"for the sake of you."* Allow that truth to settle in your heart and reassure you of His magnificent and timeless love for you. Perhaps I could rephrase that quintet of words and enable you to understand their poignancy.

Just for you.
No one else but you.
Only you.

Your God is a personal God and He loves you with a depth that defies words, travels through time, and is worth any price He had to pay. The Father sent what He holds most dear to come and buy you back from the slave market. You were rescued because of love.

It's Nice to Know

I have loved musicals since I was in second grade and first heard with my heart the wonder and whimsy of *Mary Poppins*. It seems that many musicals teach life lessons through the lyrics of the melodies framing the storyline. One of the wise lessons that has touched my soul is from the epic musical, *Fiddler on the Roof*. Do you remember the story?

Tevye, the father of three nearly grown daughters, asked his wife, Golde, one day if she loved him. She responded that she has washed his clothes, cooked his meals, cleaned his house, given him children, and milked his cow.

Golde's initial response did not satisfy Tevye, so he asked her again if she loved him. Ultimately, these opinionated, strong-willed characters finally agreed to a marital truce with the acquiescence that they "supposed" they loved one another. Tevye's closing line in the bittersweet love song is, *"After twenty-five years, it's nice to know."*

Isn't it nice to know when you are truly loved? Everyone aches to feel the human comfort of being loved by those we've invited into our hearts.

Some teenagers struggle with this greatly, wondering if their father loves them or not because of the long hours he works. They are quick to suppose their dad doesn't want to be with them and therefore he must not love them or be interested in their lives.

There are single men and women who struggle with this age-old conundrum. They assume because no one has chosen to be with them or marry them, they must be unlovable.

Many parents of grown children wonder this every day. We are sure our children are unable to understand the depth of love we still hold in our hearts even though they are now adults and living life separately from Mom and Dad. Though our children no longer need us, we still need them.

My friend, wonder no longer how God feels about you. He is passionate about spending time with you, listening to your heart, and ensuring you live a life of joy and peace. He sent your big Brother, Jesus, to die in a war zone far away from the home place just for the pleasure of your company. You are completely loved, fully forgiven, and dearly desired.

⏳   *Have you struggled with rejection?*

⧗ *Have you struggled with comparison?*

Your Attitude

Who through Him are believers in God, who raised Him from the dead and gave Him glory, so that your faith and hope are in God. (1 Peter 1:21)

Because you now know you are deeply loved and that God has been pursuing you from the foundation of the world, you should be able to embrace an attitude of faith and hope toward the Lord who loves you. There should not be a shred of disappointment in your heart when you think about God. Blame toward the Father or impatience with Him should never cross your mind. Every day of your mortal life, in all circumstances, your response to the holiness and compassion of the Father should be gratitude. You are a woman of exuberant faith and of constant hope—remember that when life tests you. Faith and hope should fill your mind, come out of your mouth, and put a spring in your step.

Faith is, quite simply, believing God is who He says He is and He can do what He says He can do. Faith is standing firm on the promises of God, knowing His Word is true. Faith is reminding yourself that God has never lost a battle yet and He is not about to do so now. This is faith:

- knowing God will work all things together for good
- believing God is on your side
- declaring the promises of God over your problems
- casting off worry and anxiety
- singing when you don't feel like it
- praying the Word of God

Hope and faith are closely aligned in definition but as I reflect on 1 Peter 1:21, I believe faith is a response of my spirit to God's love for me. Hope is the response of my emotions. Hope is my cheerleader while faith is my anchor. This is hope:

- God has good things for me.
- I have a future and a hope.
- The best is yet to come.
- God's not done yet.
- I can't wait to see what tomorrow brings.

⧗ *Write your definition of the word hope.*

⧗ *What are you hoping for?*

⧗ *Now write your definition of the word faith.*

⧗ *What do you have faith for?*

THE MIRROR

⧗ *Do you believe there is a difference between faith and hope? Why or why not?*

ETERNAL WORDS

Knowing that you were not redeemed with perishable things like silver or gold from your futile way of life inherited from your forefathers, but with precious blood, as of a lamb unblemished and spotless, the blood of Christ. (1 Peter 1:18–19)

MY PRAYER FOR TODAY

Thank You for loving me unconditionally, Father God. Thank You that Jesus was Your plan before the foundations of the world. Thank You that You sent Jesus just for me. In Jesus' name I pray. Amen.

Day 4

The Stretch of Love

One of the ways we exhibit our obedience to the Father is by loving one another. Have you discovered that sometimes love can be a stretch? It is a stretch of the emotions, a stretch of the mind, and certainly a stretch for that muscle between our pearly whites.

When it comes to loving difficult people, we must constantly remember we are obedient children. We have accepted the invitation to honor and obey the Lord in all we do and in all we say.

⧗   *Who is the most difficult person for you to love right now?*

⧗   *I want you to pause and pray the Lord will speak to your heart about loving this person as you read this chapter.*

Not a Feeling

Since you have in obedience to the truth purified your souls for a sincere love of the brethren, fervently love one another from the heart. (1 Peter 1:22)

Have you realized yet that love is a choice and not a feeling? Love is not an emotional response to another person's charming nature, attractive appearance, and easy-to-get-along-with personality. Love is an act of your will, and you must choose whether you will love the people God has placed in your life.

If you are growing in the Lord, you will grow in your love for others. If you are a woman of hope and faith you can also become a woman of love. If you are an obedient Christian, you will fervently love others from your heart. The Bible doesn't instruct you to only love the lovable people that cross your pathway. It says to love "one another." Everyone in your life is a "one another."

I can't guarantee any ease in loving difficult people, but I can assure you that loving others is a commandment from God. Often, I have allowed fractious, ornery people to bring out the worst in me when perhaps God placed these challenging folks in my life to bring out the Jesus in me.

For those of you who are in an abusive marriage or relationship, I want to pause right here and strongly encourage you to get help immediately. The Lord does not want you or your children to be abused mentally, physically, or emotionally. Confide in your pastor or in a counselor and ask for help. Go to a shelter, to the home of a trusted family member, or stay with a loyal friend. Remove yourself and your children from the behavior of the abuser.

If you are married to an addict, find help right now. Again, talk to your pastor or to a counselor and create a strategy for your safety as well as for your children's protection. The Lord wants you to be safe. You are His beloved daughter, and He cares deeply about your security.

The Lord does not want you to be abused in any respect. First Peter 1:22 is a call to unselfish behavior not a command to stay with an abuser.

⧗ *Who is the easiest person in your life to love?*

⧗ *Why is it easy to love this person?*

⧗ *Who has loved you when you were difficult to love? Perhaps you would like to thank this person or pray for them today.*

How-To

One of the most challenging aspects of loving a difficult person is figuring out how to do it. How do you love someone who is cantankerous, impatient, and critical? How do you love a "one another" who is cruel, opinionated, and grouchy? How do you do it?

First, we need to willingly and willfully let go of all evil thoughts and feelings toward this person. When an unkind or judgmental notion enters your mind, pray for the person and replace the thought with a scripture or blessing. Force yourself to make a mental list of positive qualities in this person.

Second, refuse to feel offended by this challenging person. One of my most compelling passions in life is to call a generation of women to an unoffendable lifestyle. Just as I now refuse to worry, exaggerate, or gossip, I can also resolve never to be offended again.

And finally, be proactive in demonstrating love to bothersome people. Choose to speak kindly about Mr. Demanding. Choose to tangibly bless Mrs. Obstinate. Choose to spend time with Miss Boorish. And determine to always be respectful to Sir Grumpy.

Now that you know "how to," the question is, "Will you?"

⧗ *Make a list of actions you can exhibit to the difficult people in your life.*

1. _____

2. _____

3. _____

⧗ *Now, based on Scripture, make a list of actions you are no longer allowed to take toward difficult people:*

1. _____

2. _____

3. _____

Three Words

Peter uses two very different words for love in this verse and it is important to take note of each one. He also uses another important word we must take note of in our study of this verse.

Peter employs the Greek word *phileo* in his phrase, "a sincere love of the brethren."

Phileo refers to a genuine and sincere love for brothers and sisters in Christ. This love is not simply an outward appearance or just for show, but it is cultivated and intentional.

Agape is used in the phrase "fervently love one another from the heart." *Agape* love is not possible without first knowing the love of Christ. *Agape* love is the strongest type of love because it is eternal and only retrieved from the heart of God. When your heart is beating in rhythm to the heart of the Father, you will be able to love others with the miracle of *agape* love.

All believers need to remember an important point. While I was yet a sinner, Jesus chose to love me. So, I must also choose to love those with different political persuasions, demanding personalities, and only selfishness in their hearts. I can love them because Jesus loved me at my worst.

> *But God demonstrates His own love toward us, in that while we were yet sinners, Christ died for us.* (Romans 5:8)

Not only must we love one another with the love of friendship and the love of Christ but we must exhibit love *fervently*. We don't love one another weakly or moderately but we love with pure passion and unbridled enthusiasm.

The adverb Peter strategically selected to describe how we are to love one another was an athletic term demonstrating every muscle in one's body straining and stretching. This vivid word presents the picture of an individual who is pushed to the limit and physically unable to stretch any further.[15]

The Holy Spirit understands that at times it is a painful stretch to love people and yet that is our call. Loving a demanding person will often feel painful which is the reason we need the *agape love* of the Father coursing through our souls. As you ask God for more of His love to take up residence in your heart, you will more easily be able to love others. It will still stretch you at times but your muscle of love will grow stronger and stronger.

Anything we accomplish in this world matters nothing at all unless it is about demonstrating God's love to people and proclaiming His message of salvation.

Nothing Easy About Love

Jesus, who was God in the flesh, specifically and strategically chose His twelve disciples. He could have chosen a vast number of different young men, but he chose the twelve recorded in Scripture. These were His band of brothers. They were the guys Jesus chose to hang out with while on earth. But more importantly, they were the men who would carry on for Him when He left the confines of earth to return to eternity with His Father.

Jesus did not hand-select perfect, easy-to-get-along-with guys. He didn't choose the most popular. Nor did He decide upon the most talented or educated. His companions were ordinary men, and it would take a stretch to love many of them.

Matthew was filled with pride. Our friend Peter was opinionated and outspoken. Often Peter presumed he knew better than the Lord. (I don't know anyone else like that. Do you?) Judas was weak, money hungry, and selfish. Thomas had trust issues. Apparently, John was the only disciple who was easy to love, but Jesus loved them all.

Jesus loved Peter when Peter was acting like an emotional drill sergeant. Jesus intently loved Thomas when he doubted every word Jesus said. And He loved Matthew when Matthew was acting like a childish know-it-all. I've never been able to understand how Jesus could fervently love Judas, knowing Judas would betray Him, but He did. It seems to me only Jesus can love like that. But the wonder of it is, He has provided His unconditional love as an unending resource for you and me so we are able to love every Peter, Thomas, Matthew, and Judas in our lives today.

> *A new commandment I give to you, that you love one another, even as I have loved you, that you also love one another. By this all men will know that you are My disciples, if you have love for one another. (John 13:34–35)*

Ask For It

Do you love the people Jesus has chosen to be in your life? If Jesus surrounded Himself with difficult, pretentious people, you can be sure He will do the same for you. No one is perfect, but we are given the strength to love them all.

When God calls you or me to love someone who we believe is unlovable, we are assuming the love we give others should be easy to offer. When we are called by God to love someone who is quarrelsome, it is an opportunity to die to self and sacrifice what seems important on the altar of God's greater plan. Jesus bids us to sacrifice a host of preferences and opinions. As we learn to fervently love a caustic person, we will sacrifice:

- Our time
- Our enjoyment
- Our preferences
- The words we would like to say
- Our very lives

However, what we gain by loving a peppery person is so much greater than anything we might be called upon to sacrifice. When we love a formidable person, we are becoming like Jesus. Loving a grumpy, angry individual just may lead to our finest hour.

If you are still struggling with this concept, perhaps the following thoughts will make it a bit clearer:

When you are not fervently loving someone who has been made in the image of God, it is a sin.

When you are not sacrificing to exhibit love, it is sin.

When you are not painfully stretching to love, it is sin.

Even I want to say, "OUCH!" as I write those words. This concept of fervently loving others is more than just a good idea, it is a God-idea. I, like you, must turn my hard heart toward prayer and ask the Father to forgive me for the times I have minimalized, ignored, or mistreated a valuable person. I must ask the Lord to help me bless irksome people and replace negative feelings with a miraculous response of acceptance and love. My friend, if you ask the Holy Spirit to change your heart toward someone, He will miraculously and willingly do it.

Little children, let us not love with word or with tongue, but in deed and truth. (1 John 3:18)

THE MIRROR

This was certainly a difficult lesson, wasn't it? It pierced my heart while I was writing it. I think the best thing we could do to allow the truth to saturate our hearts is to go back and read the scriptures referenced in this lesson. Ask God to give you the "want to" to love difficult people.

ETERNAL WORDS

Knowing that you were not redeemed with perishable things like silver or gold from your futile way of life inherited from your forefathers, but with precious blood, as of a lamb unblemished and spotless, the blood of Christ. (1 Peter 1:18–19)

MY PRAYER FOR TODAY

Dear Jesus, help me to love difficult people. I need Your divine assistance to wrap my heart and my actions around the challenging people in my life. Make me a conduit of Your agape love. In Jesus' name I pray. Amen.

Important Reminder

My dear friend, it is so important for me to remind you that the Lord does not want you to be abused. If you are in a marriage or a relationship where abuse is taking place, please remove yourself physically from that exposure immediately. First, find a safe place, then find a safe friend, a pastor, or a counselor who can help you make wise and godly decisions.

Day 5

The Scent of Heaven

I am one of those besotted women who adores every baby that comes within ten feet of me. I often say to my daughters and daughters-in-law, "Give me the babies. All the babies."

I'll never forget the day I held my first baby in my arms and wept for complete joy over the gift I was given. Over the next fifteen years, I was pregnant nine more times but only four ended in a live birth. The babies I was miraculously given to raise until adulthood were even more precious to my heart because of the years of stillborn babies and miscarriages.

In my mind, there is absolutely nothing as miraculous as a newborn baby, so fresh from heaven. I'll never forget creeping into my baby's room in the middle of the night and placing my nose close to their mouth so I could smell their infant breath. A baby is what loves looks like—and a baby is certainly what heaven must smell like.

⧗   *What do you think heaven might smell like? It's a fun question, isn't it?*

You Are the Miracle

Peter refers to the miracle of being "born again" two glorious times in only twenty-three verses. Let's read those verses as we begin today's lesson:

> *Blessed be the God and Father of our Lord Jesus Christ, who according to His great mercy has caused us to be born again to a living hope through the resurrection of Jesus Christ from the dead, to obtain an inheritance which is imperishable and undefiled and will not fade away, reserved in heaven for you.* **(1 Peter 1:3–4)**

For you have been born again not of seed which is perishable but imperishable, that is, through the living and enduring word of God. (1 Peter 1:23)

You, my friend, are what a miracle looks like! You are what the love of God looks like in an ordinary person, and perhaps you should even smell like heaven.

⧗ *What does the word* imperishable *mean to you?*

⧗ *What does the word* undefiled *mean to you?*

Each time Peter uses that phrase *born again*, he also uses the word *imperishable* in conjunction with it. Let's read on . . .

For you have been born again not of seed which is perishable but imperishable, that is, through the living and enduring word of God. For,

> *All flesh is like grass,*
> *And all its glory like the flower of grass.*
> *The grass withers,*
> *And the flower falls off,*
> *But the word of the Lord endures forever.*

And this is the word which was preached to you. (1 Peter 1:23–25)

The Bible is clear that you were reborn for eternity. Your life was always meant to make a timeless and imperishable impact. Although our lives and earthly pursuits are transitory or temporary, our influence is immortal. Our feelings and offenses are temporary but the fierce love we give to others is imperishable.

We usher in the abiding kingdom of God when we choose to love our enemies and encourage the discouraged.

The only way your life will exhibit the timeless influence for which you were created is when you align it with the truth-filled, power-packed, unchanging Word of God. The Word of God is an indestructible force, so let's live by it.

⧗   *Why is it important to know the Word of the Lord endures forever?*

Peter quite clearly states a few characteristics of the Word of God in these verses. He says the Word of God is:

- living
- enduring
- imperishable

The words written on the sacred pages of Scripture two thousand years ago were meant by God to have an impact today. Men like Peter, Paul, and James, who helped write the New Testament, had no idea their words, inspired by the Holy Spirit, would travel through time and still influence lives in the twenty-first century. But God knew. It has always been His plan. When Moses, David, and Isaiah were inspired by the Holy Spirit to write the portion of the Bible known as the Old Testament, they didn't realize their words would still alter lives four thousand years later. However, God knew His words were imperishable and timeless.

> **For whatever was written in earlier times was written for our instruction, so that through perseverance and the encouragement of the Scriptures we might have hope. (Romans 15:4)**

The Word Wins

As believers in Christ, we need to allow the Word of God to "win" in our hearts and minds no matter what our circumstances may look or feel like. The Word should trump our roller coaster emotions and our out-of-control thought life.

We should give Scripture the power to control our obstinate heart attitudes and corral our actions. We were born again to an imperishable lifestyle guided by the enduring words of Scripture. Perhaps a dynamic declaration for you today would be this:

> *I declare today and every day the Word of God will win in my life. I will lay down my temporary agenda for the enduring cause of Jesus Christ.*

THE MIRROR

⌛ *If you are anything at all like me, you will understand when I confess that there have been too many times to count when the Word of God did not win in my life. My emotions have won or my preferences have "out-shouted" the truth of Scripture. Why is this? What can you and I do differently so the Word will win all the time and every time?*

ETERNAL WORDS

Knowing that you were not redeemed with perishable things like silver or gold from your futile way of life inherited from your forefathers, but with precious blood, as of a lamb unblemished and spotless, the blood of Christ. (1 Peter 1:18–19)

MY PRAYER FOR TODAY

Dear Jesus, I want the Word to win in my life. Today, I declare to You that I will allow your Word to be the ruling authority in my life. Thank You, Father, for the gift of being born again into your unshakable and eternal kingdom. In Jesus' name I pray. Amen.

Week 4

The Pure Milk of the Word

Day 1

Get Rid of It!

Can you imagine not taking out the trash for two years ... or five years ... or even ten years? When the trash sits for two days in my well-covered trashcan in the pantry, the odor begins to take over the entire kitchen. The smell of yesterday's broccoli invades every corner of my home. When the trash isn't quickly and efficiently disposed of, the instant you walk in the front door the smell is all you can think about. Why would you allow the accumulated trash in your home to remain there for the next ten years? Why, indeed?

My friend, that is precisely what we do when we allow the emotional trash of yesterday's problems to pile up in our hearts. The odor becomes obvious to everyone who comes near, and no one wants to be in relationship with a woman who clings to stinky thinking. If this perspective causes you to cringe, it's time to take the trash out of your heart.

Ugly—Ugly—Ugly

> *Therefore, putting aside all malice and all deceit and hypocrisy and envy and all slander.* (1 Peter 2:1)

The Holy Spirit is offering marvelous advice in this one short verse to anyone who will listen. There are certain emotions never meant to be part of the makeup of your soul. Although inappropriate feelings might try to crawl in the backdoor of your heart, you should never welcome them into your valuable life. Peter and the Holy Spirit advise, *"Put them aside."*

If I could get just a bit graphic with you, allow me to say it this way, *"The ugly in you has to go!"*

Before my verbiage offends you, let me quickly reassure you that I am not referring to your appearance at all. My reference is directed at the emotional refuse we have allowed to remain in our hearts year after long year. I look and smell so ugly when I resist letting go of anger, envy, exaggeration, or gossip.

My personhood is trashed when I hang on to yesterday's bitterness and blame. It is then I become *ugly—ugly—ugly*. Understanding the unattractive helps us identify the appealing.

⧗   *Who is the most beautiful woman you know?*

⧗   *What makes her so lovely?*

According to 1 Peter 2:1, there are five pieces of emotional garbage the Holy Spirit requires us to dispose of. I agree with Him. *"It's time to take out the trash!"*

I Would Never Do That

Malice is the first ugly and despicable character trait Peter instructs us to put aside. Malice, in its most simple definition, is wishing something bad would happen to someone. I hope you instantly responded to this thought with the incredulous words, *"Why, I would never do that!"* Yet while we might not think maliciously in our conscious thoughts, we are often guilty of malice subconsciously.

Every time I gossip about someone made in the image of Christ I am partnering with malice. Malice also exudes a vicious and angry disposition. Sometimes, wishing harm upon others is hidden behind sweetness in a face-to-face moment while we are secretly envious or gossiping.

Put malice away, my sisters. There is no room for that type of behavior in the loving kingdom of Jesus. If the temptation is still strong, consider the following.

Whoever gossips to you will gossip of you.

—Spanish Proverb

⧗ *Have you ever exhibited malice? A simple yes or no will do.*

I'm Just Not Sure

The second word employed by Peter in the list of rancid emotional choices is the word *deceit*, and it means "to deliberately trick by misleading or lying." I wonder how many of us need to repent of this behavior and rid ourselves of its putrid bent.

Have you ever responded in this manner when your husband asked about a $200 withdrawal from the checking account? Perhaps you replied, "Well, honey, I am just not sure. I don't really remember."

Perhaps your children looked for a sweet treat and innocently ran to the pantry expecting to find those yummy chocolate cookies you bought two days ago, only to find an empty package. You might have said, "I don't know what happened to those cookies. Maybe Daddy ate them."

It's time to be done with deceit of any kind. You were born again and now your life reflects the enduring Word of God.

⧗ *Have you ever exhibited deceit? A simple yes or no will do.*

Without Wax

The third piece of trash is hypocrisy. This one is especially odiferous—its smell will curl your toes and might even trigger your gag reflex. Hypocrisy is when you say one thing but choose to do a completely different thing. Hypocritical behavior is also defined as not being genuine or sincere.

In ancient Rome, if you were a member of the upper class, the entrance to your home was graced with a huge marble statue or two. These statues were a symbol of both prominence and wealth.

However, only the extremely rich were able to afford statues completely made of marble. Those who wanted to convey the aura of wealth, while not being able to afford pure marble, owned statues with a marble façade and wax in the middle. People could not tell that these statues were counterfeit because they looked authentic.

The word *sincere* has its roots in two Latin words: *sine*, which means "without," and *cereo*, which means "wax." If you are a sincere person, you are without wax—you are genuine to your core.

My friend, throw away hypocrisy. Be a vulnerable and sincere version of you!

⧗   *Are you sincerely "you"? A simple yes or no will do.*

Green

The fourth attribute Peter demands we remove from our hearts is that of envy. Envy is desiring something that belongs to another and then becoming bitter and discontent because of it. Envy so warps our perception of reality that we are unable to be thankful for the blessings we have been given.

Some of the things women may feel envious of include the following:

- Another woman's husband
- Another woman's home
- Someone else's children
- Someone's job or income
- A friend's talent or position
- Another person's childhood or background

The quickest way to rid yourself of envy is to continually express gratitude for the blessings in your life. I keep a small journal by my bed, and nightly before I turn the light off, I note three blessings for which I am thankful that day. Gratitude keeps the green monster of envy away from my heart.

⏳ *Do you struggle with envy? A simple yes or no will do.*

Destruction

The fifth character trait that must be immediately disposed of is a mammoth issue in our culture. Every believer must immediately and thoroughly throw this evil giant out of their life.

All slander must never be tolerated in the Body of Christ. Slander is the uncontrolled compulsion to completely destroy another's reputation by gossip and rumors. In short, it is character assassination, and it is a moral crime.

⏳ *Have you ever been the target of character assassination? A simple yes or no will do.*

All the Things

As women who love the Lord and who have resolved to live our lives in joyful cooperation with the enduring Word of God, we must choose to place these horrible features far away from the grasp of our hearts. As you set these fetid practices out of emotional reach, it will often go against what you feel and what you think you are entitled to feel. But the wonderful Holy Spirit will give you the power to do this as you simply cry out to Him for help. He loves to respond to the 911 call of a woman's heart and give her the strength to do what she is unable to do on her own.

The Greek tense of "putting aside" indicates this is a decisive act of your will. We were given free will at creation; therefore, we have the power to choose what type of life we will live.

- We can choose Christ or not.

- We can choose the Holy Spirit or not.
- We can choose to obey the Word of God or not.
- We can choose to love difficult people or not.
- We can choose to worship or not.
- We can choose to take off these things or not.

The phrase *putting aside* presents the picture of stripping off a soiled garment. If you had just jogged five miles in the hot sunshine, would you wear those sweaty clothes to visit a neighbor or go out to dinner? Of course not. That's preposterous.

If you had spent the day working in your garden in ninety-degree weather, would you wear those soiled garments to go to Bible Study or to hold a baby? Of course not! That's absurd.

We should remain equally mindful of removing the emotional wardrobe we were accustomed to wearing before we knew Christ.

The Problem with Brothers

My husband and I raised a large, energetic, vocal family of five children who were separated by nearly fourteen years from start to finish. When the two older boys were playing varsity football, the three younger ones were toddlers and in early elementary school. We lived in North Carolina at the time, where the summers are searing hot and high school football is more important than sweet tea, hush puppies, and family reunions.

My boys attended a private high school known for their repeated football state championships. From the middle of July through Thanksgiving, our lives revolved around practices, sweaty jerseys, and Friday nights under the lights. My two older sons were required to attend "two-a-days" during July, in one-hundred-degree weather. I drove my boys to practice from 7:00 to 9:00 every morning and again from 7:00 to 9:00 in the evening.

The little ones, out of necessity, had to come on these forty-minute round-trip rides and they dreaded every second of it. They would beg to stay home and promised to be good, but I wouldn't hear of it. They were only babies, after all.

The reason my precious younger children recoiled at spending time in our twelve-passenger Dodge Ram van was because of the smell. There is no smell like football odor in the dog days of summer.

It was always a challenge for me to wash the football jerseys between the early morning practice and the evening practice. The turn-around was just so short and often the boys wore the same foul-smelling athletic gear to both practices in one twelve-hour period.

All the moms on the team faced the same dilemma as I did, and I'll never forget the day one of them told me this unforgettable story.

One evening as she pulled into her driveway, she told her athletic son to run upstairs and shower while she prepared a post-practice meal for him. Her boy really wanted to eat first and then shower, but she firmly told him, "Absolutely not. No boy of mine is going to sit in the kitchen smelling like a dead animal." So he ran upstairs to shower with a banana in his hand.

Her son bounded down the stairs in about fifteen minutes flat with wet hair and clean clothes on. As he dished up his plate of spaghetti and salad, this mom still discerned an odor about her seemingly clean son. What was that stench?

"Did you shower, son?"

"Yep! Sure did."

"Did you wash your hair, my boy?"

"Yes, ma'am!"

"Did you use deodorant?"

"Of course! I've gotta smell good for the girls!"

Finally, this wise mama looked her handsome son straight in the eye and confronted him, "Darling boy, something doesn't smell right. Are you sure you used soap and shampoo?"

Her man-child replied innocently, "Well, it might be my underwear. I couldn't find any clean ones, so I put my dirty boxers back on."

Is there anything in this true story that resonates with you?

Sparkling Clean

Remember, you are sparkling clean, my friend! The blood of Jesus has cleansed you from all unrighteousness so don't put your dirty clothes back on. Your family will thank you for it.

THE MIRROR

⧗ *Does your life smell? What item of trash do you need to remove from your life?*

⧗ *What did you learn from the family football story?*

ETERNAL WORDS

Like newborn babies, long for the pure milk of the word, so that by it you may grow in respect to salvation, if you have tasted the kindness of the Lord. (1 Peter 2:2–3)

MY PRAYER FOR TODAY

Dear Jesus, today I want to just stand under your cleansing shower. Wash me and I will be whiter than snow, dear Lord. Holy Spirit, I pray You will give me the strength and power to refuse a return to old habits and emotions. In Jesus' name I pray. Amen.

Day 2

Something Delicious

Healthy babies instinctively long to eat, don't they? They crave, at all times of the day and night, to breastfeed or to receive a bottle filled with nutrients and sustenance. If babies are not fed precisely on schedule, they are quick to express their agitation—loudly. Have you ever heard a baby scream who was desperate for food? A sweet, formerly compliant infant suddenly becomes panic-stricken with a red, scrunched-up face, shrieking in a tone that could break the sound barrier. These miniature people falsely assume no one will ever feed them again and they make sure everyone hears their indignation.

Satisfaction

If you are having difficulty sincerely loving people or ridding yourself of gossip, maybe you need more of the milk of the Word of God. If envy and malice refuse to be thrown out like yesterday's trash, perhaps you are lacking a daily portion of the Word of God.

> *Like newborn babies, long for the pure milk of the word, so that by it you may grow in respect to salvation.* (**1 Peter 2:2**)

It always comes back to the Word of God, doesn't it? There is nothing this side of heaven able to fill, sustain, and satisfy like the spiritual calories and joyful nutrients in Scripture. The Bible contains, in one book, timeless nourishment for our starving souls. When you fill yourself up with the Word, you are certain to experience a growth spurt in your Christian walk. Rather than just toddling through life, you will develop into an Olympic athlete of the faith. Instead of remaining a juvenile, emotionally driven believer, you will become a seasoned and wise woman who is not rattled by every little disappointment or discomfort.

Peter encourages the early church to "long" for the pure milk of the Word. I believe that same advice is exactly what he would advise for the church in the modern world. Peter was intentional in the use of the word *long* to communicate the vital necessity of craving the Word and even desperately desiring it.

We must yearn for the spiritual nutrition in the Bible more than we desire chocolate or dessert. We must wish for time spent in the Word to a greater degree than we itch to go shopping or watch a certain television show. We must thirst for the truth of Scripture more than we covet the approval of others or even spending time with our children.

⏳   *Do you have a daily quiet time? What does your daily quiet time consist of?*

⏳   *About how times per week do you read your Bible?*

Only the Best

I have a friend who is a "foodie," and like all self-diagnosed "foodies" he talks about consuming food every time we are together. He describes the recent, tender steak he just ordered at a famous restaurant, or the rich dessert his wife recently made for his birthday, or his plans for the grill this weekend. I can nearly taste every flavor he describes, and I appreciate the expertise of his palate.

Have you ever had a piece of Godiva chocolate? Once you have savored the smooth, rich delight of Godiva, cheap chocolate from the Dollar Store tastes like cardboard.

Have you ever tasted seafood straight from the ocean? Once you have feasted on fresh catch, prepared within twenty-four hours of harvest and grilled to perfection, those frozen fish sticks from the grocery store are laughable.

Have you ever sipped a hot, steaming cup of coffee whose beans were grown and hand-picked in Colombia? M-m-m-m . . . afterward, fast-food coffee tastes like sludge.

Once you have experienced the best of a certain food group, no other will satisfy the cravings of your taste buds. Cheap substitutes and empty, wasted calories just won't do. So it is with the Word of God.

> *Like newborn babies, long for the pure milk of the word, so that by it you may grow in respect to salvation, if you have tasted the kindness of the Lord.* **(1 Peter 2:2–3)**

There is no substitute for the kindness of the Lord. His eternal and timeless care and compassion are the very sustenance of our lives. The kindness of the Lord is worth savoring, devouring, and enjoying.

> *O taste and see that the Lord is good.* **(Psalm 34:8)**

When you taste of the Lord's goodness in your daily Bible reading, while you worship, or when you pray, you will partake of a delicious bite of eternity while you live on planet earth. You will experience an incomparable feast as you enjoy His presence.

> *Your words were found and I ate them,*
> *And Your words became for me a joy and the delight of my heart;*
> *For I have been called by Your name,*
> *O Lord God of hosts.* **(Jeremiah 15:16)**

The more you taste the Lord's goodness and kindness through the reading of His Word, the greater your desire will grow for the Bible. His Words will indeed become a joy to you and the delight of your heart. When we take the time, in our ordinary lives, to read the Bible, we hear the Lord call our names and we are invited to sit with Him and dine.

⧗ *What are some of the things that distract you from spending time in Scripture? Be honest.*

1. _____

2. _____

3. _____

My prayer for you today is that you will learn to fully savor your times of reading the Bible. I pray as you read the Word, you will begin to ache for it and realize that nothing else will satisfy your hungry soul.

THE MIRROR

There are three specific verses in today's reading that focus on the importance of reading and enjoying the Bible. Go back and read those verses.

⧗   *Do you look forward to reading the Bible? Why or why not?*

⧗   *What is one verse in the Bible that has deeply ministered to you over the years?*

ETERNAL WORDS

Like newborn babies, long for the pure milk of the word, so that by it you may grow in respect to salvation, if you have tasted the kindness of the Lord. (1 Peter 2:2–3)

MY PRAYER FOR TODAY

Dear Jesus, thank You for the kindness You have shown to me on the pages of the Bible. I pray You will sear Your Word upon my heart. Father, on busy days, give me the overriding desire to spend time at the table of the Word with You. In Jesus' name I pray. Amen.

Day 3

You Are a Miracle!

God never views people in the same manner that we, as human beings, assess, critique, and judge others. While people might stamp one's life as "rejected" or "failure" or "insignificant," God pronounces that very same life "precious." God's opinion, which is the only opinion that matters, says you are valuable, accepted, and cherished.

An Expert Opinion

> *And coming to Him as to a living stone which has been rejected by men, but is choice and precious in the sight of God.* (1 Peter 2:4)

Peter reminds the early, suffering church that Jesus is a living stone and although He was rejected by men, He was wonderfully chosen by God. Peter also uses a word that astounds me as I think about Peter's rugged, bold personality. Remember, Peter was a "man's man" and although his personality was tempered by the Holy Spirit, he still possessed a strength of soul that compelled him to stand unflinchingly against the cruel government of the day. The surprising word Peter employs in today's scripture is the word *precious*.

Generally, *precious* is not a word the male gender often uses.

- Grandmothers use it. "This is a precious piece of my mother's china."
- Teenage girls apply it. "Aren't they the most precious couple?"
- Mothers say it. "Isn't that little girl just precious?"

But rugged fisherman? I'm sure the word *precious* was never used by Peter or his brother, James, in their everyday banter. There was a reason they were referred to as *"the sons of thunder."*

The word *precious* Peter uses to describe God's opinion of Jesus is the Greek word *entimos*. It means, "held in honor, prized, precious."[16]

First Peter 2:4 tells us Jesus is precious to God, His Father. That piece of information, which should be so obvious, settles in my heart in sweet amazement. Somehow, the relationship between God the Father and Jesus His Son becomes even more personal and intimate as I ponder their closeness.

⧖ *How would you describe Jesus in three words?*

1. _____

2. _____

3. _____

What in the World?

As I began the in-depth study of 1 Peter that a Bible study such as this requires, I humbly responded to the Lord, *I can do this with Your strength and wisdom. But you will have to show me what a living stone is because I don't have a clue.*

> **You also, as living stones, are being built up as a spiritual house for a holy priesthood, to offer up spiritual sacrifices acceptable to God through Jesus Christ. (1 Peter 2:5)**

After Peter described the value God has for His only Son, he then expressed how the Holy Spirit views our lives. We, too, are pronounced as *"living stones"* just like Jesus.

The two words that comprise the phrase *living stone* are nearly oxymoronic—they contradict themselves when used in a twosome. Stones aren't alive; everyone knows that. Stones don't breathe, they don't grow, and they certainly don't reproduce! Isn't *that* a ridiculous thought?

As I pondered this phrase and prayed about it, I asked the Lord time after time, *Please show me what a living stone is.* Amazingly—He did. I believe I now know what a living stone is, my friend, and I can't wait to share it with you.

A Phenomenon

A living stone is, if nothing else, a miracle! A living stone has been touched by the powerful hand of God. What used to be inanimate and useless has now come to life.

This concept of viewing a living stone as a miracle can also be applied to our existence as well. Without the miracle God has wrought on our behalf, we would be no more alive than an inanimate stone. Without the interception of God, we would be unable to accomplish anything of significance—we couldn't even breathe. But God has exhaled upon our formerly dead state; therefore each of us can now be identified as a living stone. We are a living, breathing, and thriving miracle.

> ⧗   *State one specific way in which you are different from before you knew Christ as Savior.*

Gushing Miracles

A living stone is a miracle, and also a rock of abundance. You were not made alive by Christ merely to live for your own benefit. You are gloriously alive to bring sustenance and blessing to the world in which you live—much like the stone in the following verse.

> *Then Moses lifted up his hand and struck the rock twice with his rod; and water came forth abundantly, and the congregation and their beasts drank.* **(Numbers 20:11)**

You and I are living stones that should reproduce energetic water for the culture to gulp from. We are filled with the living water of Christ and must not hoard it for ourselves. We exist to splash it upon the dry, brittle souls of others.

> *He split the rocks in the wilderness*
> *And gave them abundant drink like the ocean depths.*
> *He brought forth streams also from the rock*
> *And caused waters to run down like rivers.* **(Psalm 78:15–16)**

The abundance of God is given not so we can live comfortably, hoarding the blessing of His character, and having every need supplied. You and I are alive for the wonderful purpose of sharing what we have been given with others. A living rock provides water in the wilderness. The wonder of your life is that when others thirst, you have more than enough water to share.

> **They did not thirst when He led them through the deserts.**
> **He made the water flow out of the rock for them;**
> **He split the rock and the water gushed forth. (Isaiah 48:21)**

Living rocks are filled with water so miracles will gush out of our lives when the culture is parched and dry.

⌛ *Have you ever experienced a miracle? Share about it below.*

⌛ *Have you ever prayed for someone else to receive a miracle? Share about that below.*

Loud Praise

A living stone understands that one of its primary occupations in life is to cry out in worship to the Lord who performed the miracle of its existence.

On the historic Palm Sunday when Jesus rode the colt of a donkey into Jerusalem, the crowds went wild. A multitude of worshippers spread their coats across the dusty streets as Jesus made His way toward the government that would crucify Him just days later. As the people saw the Messiah King entering the holy city, they waved palm branches in the air and cried out loudly and enthusiastically, *"BLESSED IS THE KING WHO COMES IN THE NAME OF THE LORD; peace in heaven and glory in the highest!"* (Luke 19:38).

When the Pharisees heard the stirring commotion and observed the actions of the wild throng, they sternly commanded Jesus to rebuke His disciples.

But Jesus answered, "I tell you, if these become silent, the stones will cry out!" (Luke 19:40)

Perhaps the litmus test of one's level of praise is if that stone is truly alive. Living stones will perpetually cry out in worship to the Lord despite the response of the culture. A living stone is unable to keep silent and is known by its intense and joyful worship.

As for me, I will out-shout, out-sing, and out-worship any rock in honor of my Lord on any day of the year. Will you?

⧗ *Why do you believe worship is the primary litmus test determining the miracle life you were given by the Father?*

Rocks vs. Stones

I was quite surprised to learn there is a vast difference between a rock and a stone. Rocks have no definite shape or purpose while stones are chiseled for functionality. Stones are used to build buildings and are designed to fit well into an architectural position for a specific purpose. As living stones, we must willingly allow ourselves to be chiseled by the Master Builder and to let Him fit us into a specific position in the Body of Christ. Living stones are team players, not islands set apart unto themselves.

A living stone has been fashioned and cut for God's marvelous purposes. We are not alive just to take up space but to serve the One who breathed His very life into our dormant state. My friend and fellow living stone, the Body of Christ will never be built up without your investment and your contribution. You are part of a greater work than you could ever represent on your own so make it a primary goal to be a builder in God's amazing kingdom.

⌛ *What do you believe your role might be in the Body of Christ? Perhaps*
you could list three possible assignments God has given you:

1. _____

2. _____

3. _____

Best of All

Once again, Peter is strategic and selective in the word he used to communicate the adjective *living*. There are at least three different words for life in the Greek commonly used in the New Testament.

The first word is *bios*, which refers to lifespan as well as the functions of breathing and heartbeat. Bios encompasses a person's genetics and DNA. Peter did not use the word *bios* in his description of a living stone.

Psuche life focuses on mental capabilities and what an individual learns during their tenure on earth. It might also include travel opportunities, education, and the experiences that have given wisdom to a person. Peter did not choose the word *psuche* to describe a living stone.

The third Greek word used to describe a particular type of life is *zoe*. *Zoe* life is all of the highest and best that comes from the Lord. *Zoe* life includes love, joy, peace, and hope. *Zoe* life encompasses endless blessing and delight. *Zoe* is an enthusiastic life filled with vitality. You, my friend, are a carefully selected stone, chiseled for purpose and filled with *zoe* life!

An interesting point to note is that *bios* life comes from your parentage and *psuche* life is transferred from life experiences. However, there is only one place to retrieve *zoe* life and that is straight from the heart and breath of God. I want you to note that *zoe* has nothing to do with your personality, but it is a gift from God. As you re-read the definition of *zoe* life in the last paragraph, how are you exhibiting this gift God has so generously given to you?

THE MIRROR

Now that you have completed the reading for this day, describe in your own words what you believe a living stone to be. Take a minute and pray about it and ask the Lord to show you before you write.

ETERNAL WORDS

Like newborn babies, long for the pure milk of the word, so that by it you may grow in respect to salvation, if you have tasted the kindness of the Lord. (1 Peter 2:2–3)

MY PRAYER FOR TODAY

Jesus, would You fashion me for service in the building up of Your kingdom? Would You breathe new life into me once again and give me the zoe life that only comes from You? My heart's desire is to be used in the dryness of our culture. Help me splash Your life onto everyone I meet. In Jesus' name I pray. Amen.

Day 4

Disappointments and Appointments

L ife is certainly filled with overwhelming disappointments followed by discouragement. Every day offers the potential for experiencing disillusions both large and small. We are disappointed with the weather, with the economy, and with the media. We are disappointed with education, our new haircut, and with the number on the scale.

But Peter has some wonderful news for all of us who have experienced the life of Jesus. There is one Person who will never disappoint you.

⧗ *How do you define disappointment?*

No Disappointment

For this is contained in Scripture:

**"BEHOLD, I LAY IN ZION A CHOICE STONE, A PRECIOUS CORCORNERSTONE,
AND HE WHO BELIEVES IN HIM WILL NOT BE DISAPPOINTED."**
(1 Peter 2:6)

The only foundation one should consider building a life upon is the precious Cornerstone whose name is Jesus. No one will ever satisfy you like Jesus—you can form a solid life upon that one immutable truth.

When you believe in Jesus, He will never disappoint you. Life is certainly painful at times, but Jesus never fails His children, and He never abandons you. When you are in a storm, you can expect His presence to sustain and protect you. When you are in a wilderness, you can be sure the joy of His presence and His winds of refreshing will carry you through. When life is hammering and people are taunting, He will give you His perfect peace that far surpasses all understanding.

⧗   *What is one biblical promise that brings the most hope to your soul?*

Offensive yet Precious

Jesus is precious to those of us who believe, yet to the ones who do not know Him, He is a rock of offense. What we as disciples of Christ value the most the world disdains and mocks.

> *This precious value, then, is for you who believe; but for those who disbelieve,*
>
> > ***"THE STONE WHICH THE BUILDERS REJECTED,***
> > ***THIS BECAME THE VERY CORNERSTONE,"***
>
> *and,*
>
> > ***"A STONE OF STUMBLING AND A ROCK OF OFFENSE";***
>
> *for they stumble because they are disobedient to the word, and to this doom they were also appointed.* **(1 Peter 2:7–8)**

Why are we surprised when people are highly offended by our choice to honor and serve the Lord? The world knows of no other way to respond than with ridicule. This horrible attitude is the way the world has always responded to Jesus, our precious Savior. What God's adopted children have chosen to value, the culture is sure to scorn. The morality, priorities, and disciplines priceless to the Body of Christ, the world sees as unimportant and even as putrid refuse.

My friend, we have a completely different value system than that of the world. We must never be surprised when we are scoffed at and derided simply because of our deep love for Jesus.

The world tolerates God the Father and even speaks in reverent terms about Him. They send their prayers to the Man Upstairs. However, when we speak the name of Jesus—all hell breaks loose!

⧗   *Have you ever been mocked for being a Christian? How did you respond to this ridicule?*

⧗   *Why do you believe people tolerate the name of God but disrespect the name of Jesus?*

Sad Reality

My heart aches as I read the final phrase of the passage we are studying today. I think of all the people whom I love who have chosen to mock the name of Jesus. I think about people who are dear to me and yet are disobedient to the Word and I could just weep in sorrow.

> **For they stumble because they are disobedient to the word, and to this doom they were also appointed. (1 Peter 2:8)**

Those who mock Jesus and His Word are appointed by their own choices to a certain type of doom. This scripture does not reference hell, but it does make note of "doom." As I have earnestly studied this verse, I believe Peter is teaching that when a man or woman is disobedient to the Word, there is a doom that accompanies this type of rebellion. You can be assured your loved ones were not appointed to hell by our good, good Father, but only by their personal choices.

The Lord is not slow about His promise, as some count slowness, but is patient toward you, not wishing for any to perish but for all to come to repentance. (2 Peter 3:9)

Rejecting the truth of Scripture will indeed create a life of doom and pain. Unless a person asks Jesus to forgive them of their sins and to live in their hearts, they will not spend eternity in heaven. This awful knowledge makes our job even more clear—we must tell the story of Jesus. We must love like Christ loves and tell others about His forgiveness and His death on the cross. We must stand ready to share the truth that there is only one way to heaven, through Jesus Christ.

⧗ *List the names of people you are praying will come to Christ. Pray the Lord will open the door for you to share with them the story of Jesus.*

1. _____

2. _____

3. _____

4. _____

5. _____

THE MIRROR

⧗ *What biblical truth from today's lesson was your "ah-ha" moment? Write it out below.*

ETERNAL WORDS

Like newborn babies, long for the pure milk of the word, so that by it you may grow in respect to salvation, if you have tasted the kindness of the Lord. (1 Peter 2:2–3)

MY PRAYER FOR TODAY

Jesus, I declare today You are precious to me, and I thank You that there is no disappointment in Jesus. Father, give me the boldness of Peter so I will tell others about You and Your Word. In Jesus' name I pray. Amen.

Day 5

Shout!

Often, when I read Scripture, I unsuspectingly discover a verse filled with so much vitality I just want to shout. And the truth is—sometimes I do shout while reading my Bible. I have categorized the verse we are about to study as a shouting verse—and I hope you will feel free to shout along with me.

First, however, let me tell you a story that will help you understand my reason for shouting.

When I was a senior in college, I was selected by the campus chaplain, Brother Bob, to lead all the student chaplains in my dorm. This was a remarkable honor, and I approached the assignment with both humility and intensity. Every Sunday evening, a student-led worship service was attended by nearly one thousand students at this Christian university. As a head chaplain, I served on the leadership team for the popular and life-changing gathering.

As my senior year was ending, Brother Bob called me into his office one day and asked if I would consider teaching the message on Sunday evening. They had never before asked a woman to speak, and I wasn't sure of its propriety. However, Brother Bob assured me because I was under his covering, he would introduce me and then close the service. We prayed together and I agreed to follow this beloved man's guidance.

Over the next several weeks, as I prayed over what text I would teach from, 1 Peter 2:9–10 continually knocked on the door of my heart. I realized God was speaking to me. Therefore, the first public teaching I ever presented was from the wonder and wisdom of the verses we will study together today. Now you know why I shout.

But you are A CHOSEN RACE, A royal PRIESTHOOD, A HOLY NATION, A PEOPLE FOR God's OWN POSSESSION, so that you may proclaim the excellencies of Him who has called you out of darkness into His marvelous light. (1 Peter 2:9)

⧗ *If someone asked you to speak at an event or in a class, what scripture verses would you choose to speak on?*

God's Unchanging Opinion

Have you ever wondered any of the following?

- Does my life have any meaning and purpose at all?
- Who in the world am I?
- Does my life count for anything?
- What am I supposed to do with my life?
- Who am I supposed to become?
- Am I a cosmic mistake?
- Am I misplaced in time and history?
- Do I matter to anyone at all?

My friend, it is vital to know who you are, who you were created to become, and why you are here. This timeless knowledge will give you the ability to partner with the Lord in creating the life at which angels have been known to gasp. According to today's verse, written by the Apostle Peter two thousand years ago, you are much more than you have imagined.

Your self-image is of great consequence because you were made in the image of God, your Father and Creator.

Babies don't know who they are, nor do they care. If a baby is clean, fed, rested, and loved, the little one doesn't care about their identity. Baby Christians are much the same.

Kids don't care much about their identities, either. If children have food to eat (preferably junk food), friends to hang out with, and toys to play with (preferably expensive ones), they think they are living a great life. Childish Christians are much the same.

Teenagers begin to care about their identity. They care about their gifts and talents and start to question, *Why am I here?* All of this is a healthy part of the growth process.

If you want to walk in your God-ordained destiny, then you first of all must know who He is. Then you will begin to understand who you are and what you were created to accomplish. As you yearn to learn more of who you are in Christ, I can assure you it is not a self-centered issue. Your desire is an appropriate aspect of your growth in Christ. When you know what God thinks about you, you can stand on His opinion and let Him propel you into your destiny and calling.

We are created in the marvelous image of God and it is our job to demonstrate and even promote the heart, actions, and the love of the Lord while we are employed in the family business.

> *As a child grows, they learn how to do new things such as tying their shoes, reading, and learning to ride a bike.*

⌛ *As a daughter of God, what are some of the areas of growth you have seen in your own life? As you make a list of these attributes, let me assure you that examining yourself for a growth spurt or two is not bragging.*

  1. _____

  2. _____

  3. _____

Just a Little Word

As Peter and the Holy Spirit prepare to identify who we are in the opinion of God, they begin this sentence with one tiny word, *but*. This small but powerful conjunction means "on the contrary." The preceding verse referenced those who stumble and are disobedient to the Word of God. My friend, you are the exact opposite of people who disobey the Word and thus stumble and fall.

Your identity is now determined by your relationship with the One who made you, the One who forgave you, and the One who empowers you. You have chosen, by the power of your faith, to obey the Word and to accept your appointment to abundant life.

Chosen

We have known we are chosen since the first words of this convincing epistle. However, Peter reaffirms this one facet of our relationship with the Father inside the phrase, *"But you are a chosen race . . ."*

You are chosen, so please don't reject God's Word or rebuff Him. Enjoy His presence daily knowing you are appointed. You were selected for purpose in His kingdom and it is vital you take the time to get to know Him through His Word.

My favorite day of the year is when the family McLeod gathers together for an entire day. Most of my children and grandchildren live thousands of miles away so when we do congregate it is a holiday atmosphere of the very best kind. On this annual day, it is not necessary for me to teach, instruct, or correct—I just listen. I drink in the laughter and eavesdrop on every conversation. I bask in the shared joy of this lively, wonderful brood my husband, Craig, and I created.

God feels the same way about you. He has chosen to be with you and longs for you to spend time with Him. Your identity is birthed in this non-changing reality of His wonderful choice of you!

⧖   *How does the above section change your approach to a daily quiet time spent with the Lord?*

Royalty

Peter declared that not only are you royal—but you are a royal priesthood. In the days of the Old Testament, only a priest was allowed access in the "holy of holies" of the temple where the presence of the Lord resided. Ordinary men were never allowed into this sacred and private place. However, Christ's victory on the cross changed—in an instant of time—the exclusion of common folks from entering His glorious presence. When Jesus hung on the cross, the veil in the temple was torn asunder at the very moment of His death. Now, as the royal priesthood in the family of God, we are allowed to barge into His presence boldly.

> **Let us therefore come boldly to the throne of grace, that we may obtain mercy and find grace to help in time of need. (Hebrews 4:16 NKJV)**

As a royal priest, you are invited to enter His holy presence confidently and without reserve. The blood of Jesus has made a marvelous way where before there was no way.

In Old Testament practices, one of the priesthood's duties was to bring offerings or sacrifices into the holy presence of the Lord. Now you, as a member of the royal priesthood, are also expected to bring offerings to the Lord. The first offering to bring to Him is your very life:

> *Therefore I urge you, brethren, by the mercies of God, to present your bodies a living and holy sacrifice, acceptable to God, which is your spiritual service of worship.* (Romans 12:1)

A second sacrifice is to humbly offer love to others even when it is difficult. As we demonstrate unconditional and abundant love for one another, we are offering a beautiful aroma to the Lord.

> *Therefore be imitators of God, as beloved children; and walk in love, just as Christ also loved you and gave Himself up for us, an offering and a sacrifice to God as a fragrant aroma.* (Ephesians 5:1–2)

Our next responsibility in the house of the Lord might make some people uncomfortable but we dare not ignore it. God has called us, as a royal priesthood, to offer sacrifices of money and possessions to be used to promote the gospel message. I have heard it said that salvation is free but ministry costs money. A rich and exciting aspect of your assignment as a priest is to give to the kingdom of God willingly, even cheerfully. As a priest, the question is not, *Should I give?* Instead, the question every priest should ask himself or herself is this, *How much should I give?*

> *Not that I seek the gift itself, but I seek for the profit which increases to your account. But I have received everything in full and have an abundance; I am amply supplied, having received from Epaphroditus what you have sent, a fragrant aroma, an acceptable sacrifice, well-pleasing to God.* (Philippians 4:17–18)

As a priest in the household of God, we are also required to bring a sacrifice of praise into His astounding presence. Worship is your job description—it is the very reason why you live.

> *Through Him then, let us continually offer up a sacrifice of praise to God, that is, the fruit of lips that give thanks to His name.* (Hebrews 13:15)

Not only are you a priest but you are also recognized as honored royalty by the One who made you and calls you by name. When the Father bids you to come into His presence, He might say with a twinkle in His loving eyes, "Come right on in, royal highness!"

> *The King's daughter is all glorious within;*
> *Her clothing is interwoven with gold.*
> *She will be led to the King in embroidered work;*
> *The virgins, her companions who follow her,*
> *Will be brought to You.*
> *They will be led forth with gladness and rejoicing;*
> *They will enter into the King's palace.* (Psalm 45:13–15)

As the King's dearly loved daughter, you have been given a royal robe to wear throughout your lifetime. His glory is on display in your life, and it shines forth as pure gold. The recognition of God and the display of His splendor should be revealed in your emotions, responses, heart attitudes, and your words. The majesty and kindness of God represented in your life should be obvious to everyone.

- The girl at the grocery store should look at you with admiration not because of how you are dressed but due to the joy that exudes from your countenance.

- Your unsaved husband should be amazed at how kind you are to him because you know the kindness of God leads to repentance. Kindness is a royal decree in the kingdom of God.

- Your children should want to be like you as you bring peace to every conversation and are a constant source of encouragement.

- The people with whom you work should often say, "There is a glow about you that just sparkles. What is it about you?"

The Psalmist explains precisely where the glory of God is located in our lives: *"The King's daughter is all glorious within."* The preposition *within* literally means "the wall opposite the door."[17] People will never be able to experience the undiluted glory of God in your life unless you invite them in. A second significant aspect to note in this timeless verse is that you are *"all glorious."* There should be no remnant of your former life peeking out for others to see. Everything the world has the privilege of observing in you should shine as a reflection of your royal Father!

THE MIRROR

As we complete this week of study together, ask the Lord to help you exhibit His royal character in your life. Remind yourself every morning that you are chosen to show the world who He is. It's a magnificent assignment and it is yours.

ETERNAL WORDS

Like newborn babies, long for the pure milk of the word, so that by it you may grow in respect to salvation, if you have tasted the kindness of the Lord. (1 Peter 2:2–3)

MY PRAYER FOR TODAY

Dear Father, I accept. I accept this priestly and royal assignment to bring sacrifices into Your presence. I will love others, I will give cheerfully to the Body of Christ, I will give my praise to You and I will sacrifice my very life for all You are to me. In Jesus' name I pray. Amen.

Week 5

Winning the Battle

Day 1

Celebrate and Proclaim!

We are in the middle of discovering what the Bible says about our identity in Christ. Last week, Peter stunningly declared that as believers in Christ, we are chosen and a royal priesthood. This week, we will continue gazing into the mirror of Scripture to determine exactly who we are and what we were called to accomplish in the Kingdom of Light.

> *But you are A CHOSEN RACE, A royal PRIESTHOOD, A HOLY NATION, A PEOPLE FOR God's OWN POSSESSION, so that you may proclaim the excellencies of Him who has called you out of darkness into His marvelous light.* **(1 Peter 2:9)**

Different

The third aspect of your new identity in Christ is that you are chosen, by the greatest authority in eternity, to be a holy nation. You are not holy because you are perfect, but you are deemed as holy due to your wholehearted devotion to the Lord. The word *holy*, as you may remember, means you are different.

If you are a believer in Christ and in the Word of God, you will begin to make different decisions than you were in the habit of making before you embraced this unshakable kingdom. These choices are reflected in the words you say, how you dress, what forms of entertainment you spend time with, as well as how you treat others. Your devotion to Christ makes you stunningly different in every situation and circumstance.

⌛ *List three ways a believer is different from someone who does not know Jesus Christ as Lord and Savior:*

1. _____

2. _____

3. _____

Sole Ownership

Did you know the Father has roared across the hallways of eternity exclaiming, *"She is mine! This one is all mine! She belongs solely to Me!"*

The phrase *"a people for God's own possession"* in today's verse is a term of great endearment. God is informing the powers of darkness, the magnetism of the culture, and even the angels in heaven that He has sole ownership over you and your life. Let that soak into your soul for a moment.

We all want to belong, don't we? The fact is, you are held tenderly in the heart and mind of your heavenly Father. He has informed all who might try to deceive or distract you, that no one else should ever try to kidnap you. You have entered a loving and exclusive relationship with the One who made you and calls you by name.

⧖ *When something or someone belongs to you, you are also called to lovingly take care of that possession or person. What or whom have you held tenderly in your heart and mind?*

⧖ *How have you experienced God's care in your life?*

The Rest of the Story

Now that you know the unmatched resplendence of who you are in Christ, there is a job to do.

> **So that you may proclaim the excellencies of Him who has called you out of darkness into His marvelous light. (1 Peter 2:9)**

We have an assignment, one solely ours during our moment in the history book of God. We are appointed to *"proclaim the excellencies of Him who has called you out of darkness into His marvelous light."*

We were not chosen to talk about how great we are or how horrible the people in our life might be. Rather, we are hand-selected by God to proclaim how wonderful He is in all His ways. What a significant and pivotal responsibility.

The Greek word for proclaim is *exangello*, which consists of three exciting meanings.

Exangello can mean "to tell out or forth."[18] This means we must talk about the goodness of God rather than merely think about it. And how we share matters as much as the message.

While proclaiming the excellencies that are yours in Christ, you should always be kind and compassionate rather than insulting and condescending. You can even be gentle as you share—but share you must. Live with the fruit of the Spirit (see Galatians 5:22–23), in abundance, and always tell the life-changing story of Jesus.

As you become more bold in communicating the wonder of creation, the work of the cross, and the power of the Holy Spirit, please don't project a weird or obnoxious demeanor. Be a vibrant and captivating evangelist, joyfully intent on sharing the power of God.

The second meaning of *exangello* is "to declare abroad, divulge, publish."[19] My friend, your life is a well-read newspaper with only one headline pronouncement day after day: *God is Good and Jesus Loves You!* The fact that this word includes the location of *abroad* under its meaning is an exciting reality. Abroad implies that your scope of influence is greater than you could ever dare imagine.

You could turn social media into a ministry as you reconnect with high school friends, former neighbors, and college acquaintances. I have a personal goal of impacting one neighbor a month. I learn their names, their children's names, and even the names of their dogs. I knock on their doors with homemade soup, a bouquet of flowers, or a seasonal magazine. It is my job to love them and to tell them about Jesus. My incredible Boss, the Lord, is observing, and His employees are cheering me on in my personal assignment to declare abroad.

This wide-ranging word *abroad* also implies far-reaching. Is there a teenager or college student raising money for missions? It is your kingdom assignment to help send them. If you are not going on a mission trip this year, you should be sending someone, because the greatest job you will ever have is to tell the story of Jesus abroad.

Every Christian is either a missionary or an imposter.

—Charles Spurgeon

As usual, I have saved the best for last. The final, and likely most exciting meaning of the Greek word *exangello* is "to make known by praising or proclaiming, to celebrate."[20]

My friend, as the specifically chosen, dearly cared for daughter of the King, your life has become a resounding song repeating the refrain of His inherent kindness and power. The one melody that should burst forth from your magnificent existence, times without number, is "Jesus Christ is Lord."

The word *celebrate* found hidden within the meaning of *exangello* is a strong word of feasting and trumpeting. It can literally be translated "to make much of."

Is your heart beating rapidly yet? Are you ready to jump up and down? Even on an ordinary day, the call on your life is sure and dynamic—you are called to make much of the Lord! Your life is the exciting gala event planned since the beginning of time to introduce God's love, the mercy of Jesus, and heaven's joy to a world in pain. Your life is not a pity party but it is a jubilant reception at which the guest of honor is Jesus Himself.

From Denying to Proclaiming

Do you recall from the first days of our study that Peter was the disciple who denied Jesus three times the awful night of His captivity? Peter the denier has miraculously become Peter the proclaimer. His life now shouts through the ages that Jesus is Lord!

> *But you are the ones chosen by God, chosen for the high calling of priestly work, chosen to be a holy people, God's instruments to do his work and speak out for him, to tell others of the night-and-day difference he made for you—from nothing to something, from rejected to accepted.* (1 Peter 2:9–10 MSG)

THE MIRROR

Today, I want you to make a list—let me explain. When you are planning a party you make a list of decorations, refreshments, and guests. Make a list of three vital changes you can personally make so others will feel welcome into the grand celebration of proclaiming Christ, as He deserves:

1. _____

2. _____

3. _____

ETERNAL WORDS

But you are A CHOSEN RACE, A royal PRIESTHOOD, A HOLY NATION, A PEOPLE FOR God's OWN POSSESSION, *so that you may proclaim the excellencies of Him who has called you out of darkness into His marvelous light.* (1 Peter 2:9)

MY PRAYER FOR TODAY

Dear Jesus, I commit to be a bold and celebratory proclaimer of Your light, of Your forgiveness and Your grace. I am all in! I say yes to Your word and to Your ways. In Jesus' name I pray. Amen.

Day 2

The Power to Win

Is there a temptation you continually fight more than others? Although I am not sure what your issue might be, I know even the most committed among us fights a private battle with the enemy of sin.

- Do you wrestle with sexual temptations? Or with gluttony?
- Perhaps anger is the sin that rears its ugly head and just won't let go of your tongue or heart.
- Are you critical, argumentative, and judgmental?
- Do you read books or watch movies you know are not honoring to God?
- Have you dug yourself into the red hole of debt by spending too much money on credit cards?
- Perhaps you have a problem with mental fantasy.

We all battle some type of sin or weakness, and that war often takes place in private where no one can see the struggle or help us win the fight. However, we all know God sees every secret and He longs to give us His power to win against sin. In today's lesson, Peter and the Holy Spirit are determined to equip us to conquer repeated sin issues once and for all.

⏳ *What is one way you have victoriously fought against a certain sin?*

Never

> *Beloved, I urge you as aliens and strangers to abstain from fleshly lusts which wage war against the soul. Keep your behavior excellent among*

the Gentiles, so that in the thing in which they slander you as evildoers,
they may because of your good deeds, as they observe them, glorify God
in the day of visitation. **(1 Peter 2:11–12)**

The audience of first-century Christians to whom Peter was writing had only recently come to the Lord. When this group of new believers in Christ was saved, they were instantly delivered from a lost, evil, and heathen Roman world filled with all type of horrendous sins. In ancient Rome, gluttony, adultery, homosexuality, having sex with children, and murder were all acceptable. It was a barbaric society.

The tribe of men and women living for Jesus was surrounded by a pagan environment that must have caused them to feel the lure of sin strongly. These forgiven Christians still lived among those who celebrated carnality and flaunted debauchery. It is not so far removed from the culture of today, is it?

I often remind myself that our worldly culture does not have the authority to define what is right and what is wrong in the life of a believer. If your goal is to win against the sin that bullies your life, know you will never gain victory if you justify your humanity or your culture's acceptance of sin.

⧖   *List a few sins our culture accepts but the Word of God forbids:*

1.   _____

2.   _____

3.   _____

A Flashing Light

Peter began his passionate soliloquy with a warm term of endearment to help this group of early Christians understand their leader's deep and relentless care for them. Peter calls his audience "beloved" so they will realize his words are birthed out of a heart of love and concern.

> *Beloved, I urge you as aliens and strangers to abstain from fleshly lusts*
> *which wage war against the soul.* **(1 Peter 2:11)**

The word *urge*, or *beseech* in some translations, paints the picture of a person who has something of vital importance to communicate. He or she pulls as close as possible beside the listener. When the beseecher is as near to the listener as two humans can be, then he begins to literally plead with the person to take a certain course of action. The beseecher urgently calls to the listener, imploring them to hear and follow through with the injunction.

Like a general in the faith, Peter is pulling as close as possible so he can get to our hearts today. He is earnestly begging us who live in the twenty-first century to listen to his voice and take his advice. To urge or beseech flashes a caution light designed to capture your attention—these are words of deep passion.

You're in the Army Now

Beseech is also a military word used before leaders sent troops into ferocious battles. The generals in the army called the soldiers into formation to "beseech" them. Leaders refused to hide the painful realities of war and chose to speak in a straightforward manner concerning the dangers of the battlefield and the peril that would meet the men there.

Officers were also quick to remind their troops about the glories that awaited when they won the battle they were about to face. Military leaders never dodged impending hazards, but they did come beside their troops and urged, exhorted, beseeched, begged, and pleaded with them to stand firm. These experienced military generals told their fearful troops to throw back their shoulders, look the enemy straight in the eye, and face their battles bravely and with courage.

Peter is the general speaking to the early church and to us. He wisely informs that personal discipline and an unwavering, bold warfare mentality is required to win the battle against sins the culture readily accepts.

Green Cards

Not only does Peter identify his audience as "beloved" but he also refers to believers in Christ as "aliens" and "strangers." An alien is an individual who lives among the citizens of a nation but is not a citizen himself. This alien may have met the requirements for living in the nation but he or she does not have the same rights as a legal citizen. An alien is unable to participate in activities meant solely for citizens. My friend, here on earth, you don't have your green card. You are not a citizen; you are just passing through.

Instead, we are citizens of heaven and are not allowed to participate in the activities of a lost, strange world. We are appointed to live among the citizens without acting or becoming like them.

This word *alien* is also translated as *stranger* or *pilgrim*. A pilgrim is a traveler who temporarily passes through a certain territory on his way to a final destination. A pilgrim refuses to become attached to the culture of the territory, instead staying disconnected to its language, customs, and society.

Did you have your "a-ha" moment today? Have you come to realize why we should never agree with the fluctuating culture in which we live? We are just passing through—on our way to Jesus.

MIRROR

⧖ *So often, I have bought into the mindset of the culture by reading certain books, watching movies, or agreeing with people who don't know the Lord. In what area of life has the culture impacted your mindset?*

⧖ *What should you do to change your mindset?*

ETERNAL WORDS

But you are A CHOSEN RACE, A royal PRIESTHOOD, A HOLY NATION, A PEOPLE FOR God's OWN POSSESSION, so that you may proclaim the excellencies of Him who has called you out of darkness into His marvelous light. (1 Peter 2:9)

MY PRAYER FOR TODAY

Jesus, would You cleanse my mind and heart today? Would You remove all cultural influence from my life? I want to know You, Lord, and I want to be more aware of Your Word than I am of the culture in which I live. I repent for embracing a double standard. I want You, Jesus, only You. In Your name I pray. Amen.

Day 3

Roaring Lions

There are some aspects of the Christian walk that are more fun and even encouraging to talk about than others—this is not one of them. We are discussing one of the most difficult issues that accompanies the choice to follow Christ—the issue of sin. I have read many testimonies of people who at the moment of salvation, were instantly delivered from alcohol, pornography, smoking, or other sins. Not everyone experiences that level of dramatic release.

It is sad but true that most of us continue to fight the battle with sin decades past our day of salvation. So, even though sin is a formidable topic, it is a needful one to discuss. Today we will spend a little more time lingering over the truth of the scripture we studied yesterday.

⧗   *Why is it difficult to study sin?*

⧗   *What are some of the more delightful topics to study in the Word?*

Be Intentional

> *Beloved, I urge you as aliens and strangers to abstain from fleshly lusts which wage war against the soul.* **(1 Peter 2:11)**

The four words that capture my attention as I ponder this verse are these: *abstain from fleshly lusts.* Three of those words are significant and we will study each of them one at a time.

The word *abstain* means "to deliberately withdraw from; to stay away from, to put a distance between oneself and something else."

What do you need to deliberately withdraw from? If you were a recovering alcoholic, I would advise you to stop hanging out where people drink. If you were deeply in debt due to a shopping addiction, I would say cut up your credit cards and don't sign up for any new ones. If you were married but couldn't escape the thoughts of your high school boyfriend, it would be foolish to become friends with him on social media. If, like me, you tend to eat your troubles away, I can assure you that a stash of chocolate under the bathroom sink is a horrible idea.

Our fleshly lusts are roaring lions ready to devour us. Fleshly lusts are not soft, sweet teddy bears from which we are able to obtain benign comfort. Oh, no, my friend! Fleshly lusts have eaten more than one woman alive through the course of history.

> **Be of sober spirit, be on the alert. Your adversary, the devil, prowls around like a roaring lion, seeking someone to devour. (1 Peter 5:8)**

My best advice for you today is this—stay away from starving, ravenous lions. Even better advice is to stay away from sin. Stay far, far away.

⧗ *Why do you believe Peter compares the devil to a roaring lion in the verse referenced above?*

⧗ *What do roaring lions and the call of sin have in common?*

Stagecoaches and Sin

In the old west, a flyer was posted on the window of the local stagecoach office advertising for a new driver. They had just lost a stagecoach down the side of a mountain and it was an expensive loss. The time was set for interviews and a line of men appeared by the door hours before the appointed start.

As the weary agent interviewed driver after driver, it seemed none was a good fit. This stagecoach company had formerly been known for safety, efficiency, and timely arrivals, and wanted to restore their reputation.

> "Why, I drive so fast I can guarantee I will get your passengers there a full day ahead of schedule," declared one interviewee.
>
> "I can get within inches of the edge of the cliff and never allow the stagecoach to fall over it. Ain't I still here?" boasted another.
>
> "I know so many shortcuts you never heard of," said another with a bottle in one hand as he spit tobacco out of his toothless mouth.
>
> The agent wondered if he would need to close the business. Finally at the end of the long day, a humble, young man walked in through the door.
>
> "I stay as far away from the edge as possible, sir. I may not be your fastest driver, but I will be your safest," was all this man had to say before he was hired.

My friend, heed this lesson from a now defunct stagecoach company. *Stay as far away from the edge as possible.* When it comes to sin, don't cozy up to it but walk away from it. Don't play with sin or it will play with you. And if you don't mind the mixed metaphors, playing with lions never ends well.

Higher Not Lower

The second word in our chosen phrase from 1 Peter 2:11 is *fleshly*, which means "impulses, cravings, and desires of carnal flesh; those things that appeal to our lower side."

Fleshly lusts will never enable you to become the best version of you or the you God had in mind the day He created you. Fleshly lusts will never call you higher—they bid you to come lower. When you give in to the fleshly desires that call your name, you are accepting a desire to live a low life.

⧗ *What does it mean to live a morally "high life"?*

⧗ *What does it mean to live a "low life"?*

Just One?

The third word I want to focus on from this unforgettable passage of scripture is *lusts*. It can be defined as "a person so overcome by some passionate desire that he completely gives himself over to it."

Your fleshly lust will never be content until it has completely taken over your life and consumed the best parts of you. Once you have given your flesh permission to have its way and exercise even a small amount of power in your life, it will dig its ugly claws into your heart and mind. It will wage a war for total control of your entire life. My friend, do not falsely believe you can participate in just a small taste of sin and then walk away from it. The desire to sin grows as we give in to its temporary pleasure and expands as we take a taste. Sin's growth is exponential and nearly uncontrollable without the intervention of the Holy Spirit.

When I was growing up, there was a TV commercial about an older gentleman, the devil, and a potato chip bag. Do any of you remember it? The devil came to the dapper, older gentleman with a potato chip bag in his hands and taunted, "I bet you can't eat just one!"

The older man assured him that one would be enough. However, after eating only one crispy, salty chip, the man grabbed the potato chip bag out of the devil's hands and began to devour the entire contents. The devil turned away laughing in evil glee.

Apparently, the marketing experts are aware of what you and I often ignore—it's impossible to partake of just one bite of things not good for us. If you take one bite, you're hooked.

Once the flesh is allowed to indulge in sin, the carnal nature takes over. This base drive ferociously works against you, attempting to pull you more deeply into sin until you are completely conquered by it.

It's a Battle

Peter, who never shied back from confrontation, explained precisely what these fleshly lusts would do to an unsuspecting and unprepared believer. He said they will *"wage war against the soul."*

In your specific battle against sin, you are fighting a well-trained, highly destructive enemy who has been around since the beginning of time. The Greek tense in today's verse accentuates the fact that once the flesh is allowed to express itself, it will wage continual warfare. The assault will be unending.

Strategically trained demons of sin have targeted their attack against your soul. Soul is the Greek word *psyche or psuche* and refers to a person's mind, will, and emotions. New Testament writers, by the insight of the Holy Spirit, clearly understood that the mind, will, and emotions are where Satan wages his fiercest attack against the saints of God.[21]

My friend, do not open the door to sin and welcome warfare into your soul by intentionally choosing activities that dishonor God's Word. As you succeed at abstaining from fleshly lusts, you will experience the complete freedom of safeguarding your mind, will, and emotions, preventing unnecessary battles. It is so much easier to avoid fleshly temptations than it is to uproot them, so don't think you can "eat just one."

Remember, you are a pilgrim and have no right to participate in these fleshly activities. One of the most powerful and determining choices we make as a believer in Christ is to refrain from the works of the flesh. We can never comprehend the number of horrific battles we avoid when we refuse sin the first time it knocks on the door of our heart.

MIRROR

⌛ *Well, this was certainly a graphic and difficult day, wasn't it? But even in the midst of the challenging subject matter, I know the Lord was speaking to you. What is your one take-away from this lesson?*

ETERNAL WORDS

But you are A CHOSEN RACE, A royal PRIESTHOOD, A HOLY NATION, A PEOPLE FOR God's OWN POSSESSION, so that you may proclaim the excellencies of Him who has called you out of darkness into His marvelous light. (1 Peter 2:9)

MY PRAYER FOR TODAY

Dear Jesus, I need You! I need You to help me say no the first time sin knocks at the door of my heart. I need the power of the Holy Spirit to overwhelm my fleshly desires with Your dynamic plans for my life. Thank You, Lord, that You always lead me in triumph in Christ. In Jesus' name I pray. Amen.

Day 4

His Word Is His Will

M any Christians are on a futile journey trying to discover God's will for their lives by looking in all the wrong places. You will discover the strategic plan of God for your incredible life only in the Word of God. The futility will cease when you realize God's will *is* His Word.

Once again, my friend, as we open the pages of Scripture today, we will tackle the issue of sin. It's a practical lesson and some of you may exclaim, "OUCH!" But let's continue to dig deeply for gold in the Bible, so we are able to live a life of freedom and joy.

Freedom

If you believe our government is unfair and even corrupt, remember when Peter was writing his letter. The tyrannical Nero, one of the cruelest men to ever live, was the emperor of Rome. As Peter addressed the men and women who were being persecuted, he was not speaking of a freedom-loving government which employed a system of checks and balances. Consider this as you read the following passage.

> *Submit yourselves for the Lord's sake to every human institution, whether to a king as the one in authority, or to governors as sent by him for the punishment of evildoers and the praise of those who do right. For such is the will of God that by doing right you may silence the ignorance of foolish men. Act as free men, and do not use your freedom as a covering for evil, but use it as bondslaves of God. (1 Peter 2:13–16)*

Peter did not advise the early church to worship those in authority in the governmental structure of the day but rather to show respect to political authorities. The richness of this passage is communicated when Peter reminds the church in verse 16 to *"act as free men."* We can infer this means regardless of whose government rule you reside under, you are free.

⏳ *What does it mean to "act as free men" even when you are subject to a corrupt political system?*

As Christians, we possess a freedom in Christ that supersedes all governmental systems.

- Like the godly Joseph of the Old Testament, we serve others even when we are in prison.
- Like the audacious Paul and Silas, we worship in jail at the midnight hour.
- Like Esther, we fast when our government makes a horrific mistake.
- Like Ruth, we are kind and faithful even at the darkest moment in human history.

Men and women who extract their freedom from Christ and not from a governmental document choose to serve, worship, fast, and remain faithful in the little things. A foundational belief of the Christian faith is that we are not in bondage to our circumstances. This includes the tenets of our government.

⏳ *Can you think of anyone else in the Bible who served God even when the government system was difficult or corrupt?*

I often tell young moms that what happens at your street address is infinitely more important to the plan of God than what happens at the White House, the United Nations, or at Buckingham Palace.

You and Others

Did you know Jesus is more concerned about how you treat others than how others treat you?

Honor all people, love the brotherhood, fear God, honor the king.
(1 Peter 2:17)

Honor is the bottom line in all human relationships. Unfortunately, we live at a time when the concept of honor is no longer honored. Our culture lambasts those who disagree with politically correct opinions. We berate those on social media who hold to different principles. And we cut off relationships with family members whose mindsets are contrary to ours.

Honor is simply the choice to show everyone in your life kind and respectful treatment. As you determine that honor will cast the deciding vote in your value system, you begin to listen without interrupting, use gentler words, and at times even humbly agree to disagree. When you resolve to honor others, you will respond with compassion, perhaps changing the subject when necessary. You treat others the way Jesus would if He were here today. By the way—He is here today because He is here in you. You are His chosen vessel as a conduit of honor to the world we live in.

Honoring all men and women includes:

- the people who work in the drive-through at fast-food restaurants
- the trash man, the girl who does your nails, and teachers
- postal workers, waiters, and waitresses
- your teens, young adults, and their friends
- politicians and the media
- people who vote differently than you do
- people whose skin is a different color than yours
- anyone made in the image of God

Everyone's life should be easier and less stressful because of your influence and presence. You don't have to agree with them, but you must show kindness.

Or do you think lightly of the riches of His kindness and tolerance and patience, not knowing that the kindness of God leads you to repentance?
(Romans 2:4)

If the kindness of God leads sinners to repentance, I am sure it will work for you as well.

Peter then simply but strongly states, *"love the brotherhood,"* which is the family of God. *The brotherhood* is anyone in the world who identifies as a Christian. We should proactively search out ways to show our love to all people in the Body of Christ.

⏳ *How can you make the above statement practical in your life? List three ways:*

1. _____
2. _____
3. _____

By this all men will know that you are My disciples, if you have love for one another. (John 13:35)

You and God

There are numerous blessings and privileges that belong to Christians who have chosen to cling to abundant life. One of these wonderful privileges is your invitation to fear God.

- Be amazed by His handiwork every morning when you arise.
- Look for His divine fingerprint in creation.
- Be in awe of the Word of God and treat the Bible with reverence.
- Don't take His presence for granted but enjoy it daily.

When God comes streaming into our lives in the power of His Word, all He asks is that we be stunned and surprised, let our mouths hang open, and begin to breathe deeply.

—Brennan Manning

And Then There Is the King

Peter finishes today's focal verse with the admonition to *"honor the king."* This may mean president, prime minister, or some other leadership title, depending on where you live. Before you respond with resistance, remember God's will is found in His Word. We obey God's Word rather than our emotions. We are women who value honor and therefore we can give honor to anyone who is made in the image of God—including political leaders of our day. We don't have to agree with them, but we must honor their position and authority.

MIRROR

Make a list of political figures you will commit to pray for through the rest of this study. I encourage you to list the names of men and women with whom you especially disagree and then pray for them daily.

1. _____
2. _____
3. _____
4. _____
5. _____

ETERNAL WORDS

But you are A CHOSEN RACE, A royal PRIESTHOOD, A HOLY NATION, A PEOPLE FOR God's OWN POSSESSION, so that you may proclaim the excellencies of Him who has called you out of darkness into His marvelous light. (1 Peter 2:9)

MY PRAYER FOR TODAY

Jesus, thank You for the trusted roadmap of the Word of God. I will take this section to heart and show honor to people in my life with whom I disagree. I will be kind to people of all races and political persuasions. And Father, I honor You with my very life. In Jesus' name I pray. Amen.

Day 5

A Nugget of Gold

Today's lesson will be a short one but don't be fooled by its length. You will find a nugget of gold in this lesson that just might provide a piece of wisdom you have ached for. And remember, God's will is always found in His Word so we must submit to it!

It's time for a self-examination:

1. *Do you believe the Bible is the inspired Word of God?*

2. *Are you building your life on the principles found in the Word?*

3. *Is there a principle or command in the Word you struggle with? Write it below.*

In the Army

Once again, Peter utilized a military term to describe a particular concept of Christian living. He presented a strategy for the workplace that is at once practical and life-giving.

> *Servants, be submissive to your masters with all respect, not only to those who are good and gentle, but also to those who are unreasonable. For this finds favor, if for the sake of conscience toward God a person bears up under sorrows when suffering unjustly. For what credit is there if, when you sin and are harshly treated, you endure it with patience? But if when you do what is right and suffer for it you patiently endure it, this finds favor with God.* (1 Peter 2:18–20)

The word *submissive* is a military term that refers to *a flow of power, an arrangement of superiority and a voluntary giving in and carrying a burden for someone else.* A submissive spirit is especially applicable for your work environment as you seek to be an excellent employee whose goal is not just to earn a living but also to honor the Lord. If you have a boss or a team leader, be submissive with your words, energy, and your work ethic. When you embrace this type of heart attitude at your job, you will find favor with God.

Peter instructed the servants who were recipients of his sage advice that even if they were treated harshly, they were to remain patient and submissive. And Peter wasn't the only leader in the early church who heard this same instruction from the Holy Spirit and then communicated it. Paul also wrote very similar words:

> *Slaves, in all things obey those who are your masters on earth, not with external service, as those who merely please men, but with sincerity of heart, fearing the Lord. Whatever you do, do your work heartily, as for the Lord rather than for men, knowing that from the Lord you will receive the reward of the inheritance. It is the Lord Christ whom you serve.* (Colossians 3:22–24)

Your Main Job

The most important mindset you embrace in the workplace should reflect that of an employee who remains kind, faithful, and respectful. God will show you His favor when you conduct your business in such a manner. Isn't it wonderful to know the Lord is interested in the details of our everyday lives? One of His main concerns is how you treat others and how you exhibit His character at work.

The manner in which you carry yourself in the workplace is not your ticket into heaven—only the blood of Jesus applied to your life does that. However, choosing to live your life faithfully every day of the week, not just on Sundays, will capture God's attention as well as His favor. God has entrusted difficult people and demanding bosses to His children so we will exhibit God's love and shine His light into their lives. Your main career is not your job, it is how you treat the people with whom you spend your waking hours.

⌛ *If you work outside the home, list three people you will pray for in your workplace. If you don't work outside the home, list three people you used to work with or who you currently have contact with who need Jesus. And then be kind to them, knowing the kindness of God leads to repentance.*

1. _____

2. _____

3. _____

THE MIRROR

⌛ *Do you have any regrets about how you lived your life in high school or in a former work environment? Have you asked the Lord to forgive you? Why don't you also ask Him to give you another chance with people so you can lead others to Christ.*

ETERNAL WORDS

But you are A CHOSEN RACE, A royal PRIESTHOOD, A HOLY NATION, A PEOPLE FOR God's OWN POSSESSION, so that you may proclaim the excellencies of Him who has called you out of darkness into His marvelous light. (1 Peter 2:9)

MY PRAYER FOR TODAY

Dear Jesus, I long to be used by You. I am saying yes to You today in the workplace, in my neighborhood, at my church, in public places, and in my home. Open doors for me to make hell smaller and heaven bigger. In Jesus' name I pray. Amen.

Week 6

Purpose and Calling

Day 1

In Every Situation

How many of us have wondered what our purpose in life might be? Innumerable times I have questioned if everyone else had a God-ordained purpose except me. I looked at others, observed their call to accomplish great things for the kingdom of God, and felt left out. I was wrong, of course, and got caught in the mire of comparison. I am so grateful Peter wrote the verse below to a suffering church and to me.

⧗ *Do you believe God has a specific purpose for each one of us? Why or why not?*

⧗ *What do you believe your purpose in life is?*

A Specific Purpose

> *For you have been called for this purpose, since Christ also suffered for you, leaving you an example for you to follow in His steps. (1 Peter 2:21)*

This verse rips the comparison rug out from under my insecurities as I remind myself that every word in the Bible is for me. My purpose is to follow the example of Jesus Christ. In every situation, in every experience of suffering, and in every trial, I am to follow in His footsteps. In every joy and in every painful experience, my specific call is to follow the One who loves and protects me.

> *For you have been called for this purpose, since Christ also suffered for you, leaving you an example for you to follow in His steps, WHO COMMITTED NO SIN, NOR WAS ANY DECEIT FOUND IN HIS MOUTH; and while being reviled, He did not revile in return; while suffering, He uttered no threats, but kept entrusting Himself to Him who judges righteously; and He Himself bore our sins in His body on the cross, so that we might die to sin and live to righteousness; for by His wounds you were healed. For you were continually straying like sheep, but now you have returned to the Shepherd and Guardian of your souls. (1 Peter 1:21–25)*

Jesus set a perfect and powerful example for behavior before us. He exemplified correct responses to every situation in life. Although Jesus was blasphemed, reviled, and cursed, He never fought back. Nor did He allow Himself to be dragged into a war of words. And honestly, if there was a communication battle, Jesus would have won every time.

Jesus knew He would win a war of words because He *was* the Word (John 1:1,14).

> *And the Word became flesh, and dwelt among us, and we saw His glory, glory as of the only begotten from the Father, full of grace and truth. (John 1:14)*

Despite possessing the wisdom of the ages and superb verbal skills, Jesus didn't correct or one-up His accusers. Upon His capture, though He could have verbally retaliated in triumph, thus saving His own life, Jesus stayed quiet. We can learn from His example. Likely, there are times you and I need to stay quiet as well.

When you or I enter a war of words on social media or in our personal relationships, we don't have Jesus' assurance of a verbal win. Yet we are often foolish enough to fight intensely. I've realized I need to be like Jesus in terms of persecution and suffering. When I feel cornered, I need to keep my mouth closed and know He is fighting every battle on my behalf.

⏳ *Do you tend to talk too much or withdraw when you are going through a difficult time?*

Just Like Him

There are two principles of change noted in today's focal passage that offer the how-to instruction we need.

When faced with intense difficulty, I first need to be less like me and more like Jesus. Anyone can respond in a sweet and loving way when all is well in his or her personal life. We must remember our specific calling is to act like Jesus when our world has just fallen apart. We are to demonstrate the character of Christ during dark, difficult days.

The second principle Peter directs us to when faced with formidable days reminds us to consider the words we speak. The Holy Spirit can evaluate the sincerity of our desire to be like Jesus by the words that come out of our mouths when we are in a storm of suffering. When it becomes dishearteningly obvious that your circumstances are about to be torn apart by a tornado of gargantuan proportions, have you been known to fuss, whine, or complain? Or do you declare you will trust the Lord no matter what is going on?

Do you insist on repeatedly telling your side of the story when you are in a searing relationship fire? Do you post all the details of your health battle on social media? Or do you post scriptures focusing on the goodness of God when times are tough?

These are exacting principles to follow but the benefits are astounding. How much do you desire to be like Jesus? The proof will be seen in the words you withhold or speak.

⏳ *What does it mean in a practical sense to "trust the Lord"? What actions might this entail?*

The Best Place Possible

Rather than entering into verbal debate during times of persecution or suffering, you must keep entrusting yourself to the One who judges righteously. The words *"kept entrusting"* from 1 Peter 1:21–25 can also be translated as "drawing very close." If you long to be like Jesus, then you will do what Jesus did at the worst moment of His life. You will keep your mouth closed and stay in a close and trusting relationship with the Father. As you choose to trust Him, you are acknowledging that He is the One with true power in any situation confronting you.

In every circumstance, we must immediately relinquish our circumstances over to the One who is more than able to right a wrong. Even today, our caring Father heals the sick, encourages the discouraged, and writes the end of our stories with His goodness.

If you have found yourself in a situation that seems unfair or unjust, draw as close as you can to the Father and rest in His compassion. The power of committing your circumstances into His capable hands cannot be overstated. As you acknowledge the timeless truth that God desires peace and safety for your life, you will also know He is trustworthy.

If you are currently experiencing a circumstance that seems undeserved, you have two determinants from which to choose:

- You can become angry and bitter. You can talk too much. You can build a wall between you and the Lord. You can question His character and His goodness.

- Or you can choose to believe your good, good Father will have the final word and He is working behind the scenes on your behalf. You can draw close to Him through reading the strengthening Word, by listening to comforting worship music, and by praying fiercely for others. You can make a list of the things for which you are grateful even in the middle of the storm.

Jesus had no other choice but to trust His Father. What other choice do you really have?

MIRROR

⧖ *Think of a time when you experienced a relentless and damaging storm in life. How did you respond? List three beneficial choices you made and also three poor choices you made during that time. Then, list three things you will do differently next time.*

Beneficial:

1. _____

2. _____

3. _____

Poor:

1. _____

2. _____

3. _____

Next Time:

1. _____

2. _____

3. _____

ETERNAL WORDS

Your adornment must not be merely external—braiding the hair, and wearing gold jewelry, or putting on dresses; but let it be the hidden person of the heart, with the imperishable quality of a gentle and quiet spirit, which is precious in the sight of God. (1 Peter 3:3–4)

MY PRAYER FOR TODAY

Jesus, today I thank You that the trials in life give me the opportunity to be more like You. I pray You would help me close my mouth when I don't like my life and that You would welcome me into the joy of Your presence in these awful moments. Thank You for loving me and taking care of me. In Jesus' name I pray. Amen.

Day 2

Women and the Gospel

Before we begin to study the next few verses, I'd like to ask five vital questions. Affirming your faith will enable a teachable spirit as we move ahead. Please consider each question carefully and be honest with your answers.

1. *Do you believe the Word of God is true for every generation?*
2. *Do you believe the Bible is applicable to your life today?*
3. *Do you believe the Word of God presents a life of freedom and not legalism?*
4. *Do you believe that when you obey the Word your life becomes more abundant and therefore more joyful?*
5. *Do you believe the Word of God is timeless?*

Jesus and Women

When Jesus came, He revolutionized how women were treated and were even thought of. Prior to the life of our Savior, women were objectified and used as slaves by men for sexual pleasure and physical labor. Women were expected to be seen and not heard—their worth was no greater than the family cow.

However, when Jesus arrived, a dynamic transformation began for the female gender. For instance, He called the woman with the issue of blood "daughter." While others rejected her, Jesus embraced her with love and concern. He welcomed women to join the men around Him as He taught eternal lessons of truth and hope. Women accompanied Jesus and the disciples as they traveled from town to town. No teacher had ever done this before. Jesus demonstrated, by example, the value and worth of women in His eternal kingdom.

In my heart, I believe the most wonderful change of all came on the morning of Christ's crucifixion. At the tomb, early on the day when Jesus rose from the dead, women were first to receive instruction from the angel of the Lord to go and tell of the resurrection miracle.

The angel said to the women, "Do not be afraid; for I know that you are looking for Jesus who has been crucified. He is not here, for He has risen, just as He said. Come, see the place where He was lying. Go quickly and tell His disciples that He has risen from the dead; and behold, He is going ahead of you into Galilee, there you will see Him; behold, I have told you."

And they left the tomb quickly with fear and great joy and ran to report it to His disciples. And behold, Jesus met them and greeted them. And they came up and took hold of His feet and worshiped Him. Then Jesus said to them, "Do not be afraid; go and take word to My brethren to leave for Galilee, and there they will see Me." (Matthew 28:5–10)

As we now ponder the theme of the following verses, remember there was no disdain in the heart of Jesus for women. He elevated females to a valuable place in society.

⧗   *Do you feel as accepted and useful as men in the Body of Christ? Why or why not?*

No Rights At All

During the first century, when Peter wrote to the early church, women had no rights at all. If a woman was caught in adultery, her husband could murder her. On the other hand, if a man was caught in adultery, his wife wasn't even allowed to confront him. This one example communicates the vast difference between men and women at that time.

A woman was owned by her husband, just as he owned sheep and goats and property. A wife was not allowed to leave her husband, but he could dismiss her without any explanation at all.

If a man became a Christian, he automatically brought his wife into the Body of Christ. However, if a woman became a Christian, it produced acute problems in the marriage. Her husband could divorce her, preventing her from seeing her children again. There was no alimony, and she would be left homeless with no financial support.

Crucial Reminder

Before we begin the next section, let me remind you of one vital truth. We spoke of this in a prior lesson.

- If you are in an abusive relationship, remove yourself immediately. Whether physical, sexual, emotional, or mental, reach out to the leader of this Bible study and she will help you.

- If your spouse is abusing your children, remove yourself and your children now. Regardless of the form of abuse, whether physical, sexual, emotional, or mental—all are unacceptable. Speak with the leader of this Bible study and she will provide guidance.

- If your spouse has an addiction to drugs, alcohol, or pornography, find immediate help. You may also need to leave.

As I teach on the principles of submission in marriage, I must make certain that women do not mistakenly believe they need to stay in an abusive marriage. You will understand as you read further into this chapter what submission is and what it is not.

Women and Marriage

As we study what the Bible says about marriage, I'd like to remind the single women of a crucial point. I believe that who you choose to marry is the second most important choice of your life—trumped only by your decision to follow Christ. The man you wed will completely change every area of the life you embraced as a single woman. I pray the concepts presented in this section will come alive in your heart and prepare you as the loving and fulfilled wife God has called you to be. My single sisters, do not ever marry a man whose decision-making is void of Christlike wisdom.

I dated several young men prior to my relationship with Craig, the wonderful man I married over four decades ago. As I observed Craig's life and his heart for ministry, I knew I could trust him and therefore could submit to him as his wife. I have no regrets in my decision.

If you are single, these are the consequential matters you must evaluate before you say yes to an engagement ring:

- Is this man a believer in Christ? Ask about his salvation experience and share about yours. You must not enter into marriage with an unbeliever.
- Is he kind? To you? To his parents? To his siblings? To children?
- Do you pray together? Is he willing?
- Is he unselfish?
- Do you trust his decision-making process? Is he wise or impetuous?
- Does your relationship with him draw you closer to the Lord or does it cause you to ignore or minimize your faith?
- Is he pressuring you to enter into a physical relationship outside marriage?
- Is he easily angered or is he calm and patient?

Perhaps you are a widow, and as such, you might harbor wonderful memories or enormous regrets concerning your marriage. If you have lost your spouse, these are the assignments I would ask you to consider as we study biblical principles concerning marriage:

- Pray for the young wives who are involved in this study with you.
- Pray for the women who are struggling in their marriages.
- Take good notes and pray the Lord would allow you to biblically mentor younger women.

Perhaps you are divorced and filled only with regrets about the choices you made concerning marriage. Maybe you feel victimized by a relationship that upended your life. If you have found yourself in this group of women, the most life-giving choice you can make is to pour your regrets out to Jesus. It's a new day and He can infuse you with hope, blessing, and purpose. Offer your life to the Lord for service in His kingdom and allow Him to wrap His arms of mercy and grace around your broken heart.

If you are married, prepare yourself to become the wife you have always wanted to be. You can stand assured that God is at work in you for His good pleasure.

⌛ *What is your marital status?*

⌛ *How does the advice in this "Women and Marriage" section help you in the season of life you are currently in?*

Read and Pray

We are now ready to prayerfully read 1 Peter 3. However, we will wait until tomorrow to dig deeply into the Scriptures. For now, I would like you to read the following and ask the Lord to speak to you personally before tomorrow's study.

> **In the same way, you wives, be submissive to your own husbands so that even if any of them are disobedient to the word, they may be won without a word by the behavior of their wives, as they observe your chaste and respectful behavior. (1 Peter 3:1–2)**

THE MIRROR

I have two mirror assignments for you today. I believe both will be beneficial and beautiful.

First, write your definition of the word marriage.

Second, write your definition of the word family.

ETERNAL WORDS

Your adornment must not be merely external—braiding the hair, and wearing gold jewelry, or putting on dresses; but let it be the hidden person of the heart, with the imperishable quality of a gentle and quiet spirit, which is precious in the sight of God. **(1 Peter 3:3–4)**

MY PRAYER FOR TODAY

Lord, prepare my heart for the teaching this week. I pray my spirit will be soft toward Your will and Your way. I know Your plans are always the best. Even when I don't understand Your Word, Lord, I am committed to obedience with joy. In Jesus' name I pray. Amen.

Day 3

The "S" Word

When our third son, Jordan, was about six years old, he had spent the day playing with Jonathan, who was one of the elder's sons at our church. Craig, my husband, was the pastor of our small but growing church. Craig was driving Jonathan home and listening to the little boys visit in the back seat. These two boys were filled with life, enthusiasm, and verbal excess. It was delightful to hear what they might say next.

Jonathan asked Jordan if he liked to watch movies. (Now remember, this was during the days of VHS and movie rentals. In our household, every movie we watched was benign and family friendly.) Jordan, while swinging his feet and finishing his popsicle, replied, "Yes. We even get to watch movies with the 's' word and the 'd' word."

Craig tried not to gasp out loud. After he dropped Jonathan off, my husband immediately began questioning Jordan. Craig tried to stay nonchalant in approaching this sensitive topic. "Jordan, can you tell me what the 's' word and the 'd' word are?" he patiently queried.

"Yes, Dad," Jordan exclaimed in his signature croaky voice. "You know—stupid and dumb."

Phew!

It's time for us to talk about the "s" word that many of us falsely believe is horrible and outdated. The truth is, *submission* is timeless.

Submit to Submission

> *In the same way, you wives, be submissive to your own husbands so that even if any of them are disobedient to the word, they may be won without a word by the behavior of their wives, as they observe your chaste and respectful behavior.* (1 Peter 3:1–2)

Submission is one of the most misunderstood words in Christianity and it might just be the least popular teaching in the Body of Christ. As Americans, our backs bristle and our tempers flare when anyone threatens to minimize our well-loved independence. When twenty-first-century women even hear the word *submit*, they respond in various ways. The most common concerns are these:

"You mean I don't get my own way?"

"You mean I am not always right?"

"You mean someone is demanding I die to self?"

As we begin to dig for gold in today's well-known but controversial verse, I can assure you that submitting to submission may be the greatest choice you ever make.

⧗   *How do you define submission?*

⧗   *How does the word submission make you feel?*

⧗   *Do you believe wives submitting to their husbands is old-fashioned—or does submitting apply to marriage in the twenty-first century?*

What It's Not and What It Is

Submission is not blind obedience nor is it accepting abuse in any form. Submission does not imply inferiority to another person or to a different gender. Submission is not following actions that dishonor God, nor is it being led astray from the principles found in Scripture.

Jesus was equal with God yet submitted to death on a cross because of its powerful, history-defining outcome. The clear example of Christ's willing sacrifice, giving His life for us, verifies there will be times when submission is not pleasant or easy.

Submission, when viewed through the upside-down lens of the kingdom of God, is a noble action of influence and distinction. The Bible reminds us that a servant in God's kingdom is greater than his or her master.

> *But the greatest among you shall be your servant. Whoever exalts himself shall be humbled; and whoever humbles himself shall be exalted.* **(Matthew 23:11–12)**

As we consider the New Testament admonition for the wife to submit to her husband, we must change the way we think about this word. Submission in no way communicates that the wife is less important than the husband. Submission is simply a call for a woman to be more like Jesus.

Submission is fitting yourself to your husband's leadership and therefore respecting his God-given authority. Submission is willingly following your husband's guidance and acknowledging that the husband, as ordained by God, is the head of the home. Submission can also be viewed as accepting the relationship roles God has designed with cheerful and voluntary selflessness.

The word *submission* can also be translated as *yield*. If you are a driver, you know yielding to other cars and drivers can prove a life-and-death matter. We yield to traffic to avoid a collision. We submit in the home to similarly avoid an emotional collision. This is a concept with which I am well experienced.

My husband and I offered premarital counseling as well as pastoral family counseling for years. I often explained the roles within marriage by using the analogy of a husband as the head of the home while the wife is the heart of the home. I then asked these two follow-up questions:

⏳ *Which would you rather live without—your head or your heart?*

⏳ *Which is more important—your head or your heart?*

Even as I ponder this illustration after forty-five years of marriage, I can assure you that wives are not more important than husbands in the scheme of God's plan. Conversely, husbands are not more vital than their wives. We are different—gloriously so—with contrasting purposes and job descriptions.

Serving your husband and fitting yourself to his leadership is the sweet roadway to greatness in the family of God.

⏳ *If you are currently married, how can you fit yourself to your husband's leadership?*

⏳ *If you are not married, what married couple can you pray for today?*

⧗ *If you want to be married, make a list of three things you would like the Holy Spirit to do inside of you before you wed.*

1. _____
2. _____
3. _____

The "S" Word Is for Everyone

Women, in case you are still dealing with frustration over the call to submission, I can assure you submission is not a gender issue. Submission is for all of us who have chosen to align our lives with the abundant call of Scripture.

***And be subject to one another in the fear of Christ.* (Ephesians 5:21)**

The phrase *submit to one another* is on each one of our job descriptions whether we are single or married, male or female. Submission was God's idea. We must lay down our twenty-first-century independence and admit the Father knows best. Submission is the call to voluntary selflessness. The Lord is poignantly and powerfully aware of what is required for His children to build successful and meaningful relationships.

God is gently whispering in your ear today. Do you hear Him? He is saying: *Demanding your own way is not best. Choosing to remain stubborn and willful is not best. Insisting on spouting your opinions, beliefs, and preferences is not best. My way is the best way.*

Peter does not encourage wives to become doormats, nor is he saying the insights and desires of a woman are meaningless in a marriage. He is simply urging wives in every generation to take their place in marriage as their husband's chief supporter, helper, best friend, and loving partner. People in all walks of life are transformed when someone they care about gives a word of encouragement, supports them in their endeavors, and makes their life easier. This is submission in its purest and most unselfish form.

⧗ *What are some reasons women have a difficult time understanding the concept of submission in marriage?*

1. _____
2. _____
3. _____

But You Don't Know My Husband

As I read the words of Peter, it always interests me that this particular strategy of submission specifically targets women whose husbands don't know the Lord. I'll admit I would love to have a conversation with Peter and the Holy Spirit about why so many women are drawn to unbelieving men. But I, too, must lay down my opinions and concerns and trust the Bible is eternal and inerrant.

If your husband is not a believer, or is difficult to get along with, perhaps this practical outline based on biblical mandates will help you:

- Be sweet and kind with your words and with your tone of voice.

- Don't be argumentative or quick to disagree.

- Smile often and encourage your husband daily.

- Serve your husband with loving-kindness.

I think the following two verses, found other places in the New Testament, will prove beneficial to all of us who are married. If you are unmarried, these verses will improve all your relationships:

> *But encourage one another day after day, as long as it is still called "Today."* (Hebrews 3:13)

> *This you know, my beloved brethren. But everyone must be quick to hear, slow to speak and slow to anger; for the anger of man does not achieve the righteousness of God.* (James 1:19–20)

⧗ *Based on today's reading so far, what do you hear the Holy Spirit saying to you?*

Evangelism in the Home

Peter encourages women from every juncture in history to be submissive to their husbands for the sake of evangelism.

> *In the same way, you wives, be submissive to your own husbands so that even if any of them are disobedient to the word, they may be won without a word by the behavior of their wives, as they observe your chaste and respectful behavior.* (1 Peter 3:1–2)

The phrase *"if any of them are disobedient to the word"* implies someone who refuses to be persuaded. Your words may not persuade your husband to embrace Christ but perhaps your lifestyle will do what your words have failed to accomplish. This is a verse with a promise included in its heart, *"they may be won without a word by the behavior of their wives."* My friend, you may win the challenge by positively influencing your husband without ever saying a word.

The word *behavior* means "how a person rises up and sits down; goes in and goes out; turns this way or that way." How you choose to behave in every situation is vastly more important than the words you speak. Your godly life is the greatest pulpit from which you present a mighty sermon.

Did you realize your husband is watching you and evaluating your faith? The reason we are to submit and believe God for a difference in the lives of our husbands is that husbands *observe your chaste and respectful behavior.* Your husband has his eye on you and is amazed when you remain happy and content, despite his gruffness or indifference. He notices how you respond to the children, to his mother, and to his behavior. Men notice it when their wives are simply awesome.

A wife's godly conduct is the most influential, powerful, and essential sermon she could ever preach to her husband. Your cheerful countenance, your patient words, and your daily wisdom make a difference in your marriage and in your home.

THE MIRROR

I know for some women, this lesson was a difficult one. If you are in a challenging relationship, I am so, so sorry. I hope you find a prayer partner who will pray for your marriage and for your husband.

I know for some of you, submission is still a difficult word. If that is so, pray the Holy Spirit will speak to you about His plan for marriage.

What component of the word submission *most resonated with you?*

ETERNAL WORDS

Your adornment must not be merely external—braiding the hair, and wearing gold jewelry, or putting on dresses; but let it be the hidden person of the heart, with the imperishable quality of a gentle and quiet spirit, which is precious in the sight of God. (1 Peter 3:3–4)

MY PRAYER FOR TODAY

Jesus, I want Your way more than I want mine. I pray You will give me Your grace to act like You in my home. I pray You will give me Your heart about submission. In Jesus' name I pray. Amen.

Day 4

Silent Preaching

Who is the most beautiful woman you have ever met? Was it because of her gorgeous designer clothes or perfectly styled hair? Was she attractive due to her slender figure? Her makeup and astounding eyelashes? Her manicured nails? I feel certain most of us would agree that the most beautiful and becoming woman we have ever encountered possessed a rare presence not birthed from outer accessories but from an inner grace.

As much as I love teaching the deep truths from Scripture, I must tell you this section of 1 Peter is among my favorite passages to share with women. It will make a profound difference in each one of us when we truly understand the loveliness of a gentle and quiet spirit.

⧗ *Who is the most beautiful woman you have ever met?*

⧗ *What has made this woman attractive?*

Louder Than Words

Loveliness in the soul of a woman presents a silent sermon not easily ignored. Actions speak so much louder than words ever could—especially in the heart of family life. Words can sound preachy and even obnoxious. Conversely, purposeful, kind actions demonstrating the reality of the gospel of Christ are warmly welcomed and atmosphere determinants. Strong words can stir up anger and thus cause division, but intentional and heartfelt responses cultivate trust and change.

If your husband has not yet embraced Christ, strengthen your marriage by choosing not to preach but to love deliberately and to live with grace. You can trust God to open the door for you to share your faith in an appropriate manner at the right time, but your strongest witnessing approach will be demonstrated by becoming a loving and kind servant in your home. Remind yourself often that it is in serving others where we experience true greatness in God's economy. A wife who preaches at people in her home will never discover the result she desires. However, the Holy Spirit is an expert at pursuing those who are being diligently prayed for.

⌛ *Who are you praying for in your family? Write their names below.*

1. _____

2. _____

3. _____

4. _____

5. _____

Be-YOU-ti-ful

Although it might seem awkward at first, let's begin by studying the final verse of the following passage.

> *Your adornment must not be merely external—braiding the hair, and wearing gold jewelry, or putting on dresses; but let it be the hidden person of the heart, with the imperishable quality of a gentle and quiet spirit, which is precious in the sight of God. For in this way in former times the holy women also, who hoped in God, used to adorn themselves, being submissive to their own husbands.* (1 Peter 3:3–5)

One of the most intriguing promises found stashed away in this pertinent series of verses is this: *submission will make you beautiful.* Isn't that interesting? The Holy Spirit states in 1 Peter 3:5 that the women in ancient days utilized submission as a way of becoming more beautiful.

The word *adorn* found in the final phrase of this passage means "to ready, to prepare, to embellish with honor, to gain honor." It is the Greek word *kosmos* from which we get our modern word *cosmetics*. The implication is when you willingly submit or cooperate with your husband, you are making the choice to embellish yourself with honor.

Women in the days of the early church desired to feel attractive just as women do in the twenty-first century. During the days of the first century there was an obsession with one's appearance just as there is today. Women two thousand years ago were fixated on flamboyant hairstyles and spent vast amounts of money on cosmetics, expensive jewelry, and lavish clothing. Although they didn't have glamorous movie stars setting the standard for them, the struggle for outward beauty was much the same as it is today.

Peter is very careful how he phrases this admonition to women and inserts the word *only* or *merely* into its meaning. It's not a Bible command for women to forfeit clothing, makeup, or jewelry; however, we must not falsely believe those are the additives that make us into the most beautiful version of self. It is not a sin to look attractive or to invest time and energy into appearing your best. However, always remember your eternal beauty is derived from an inner adornment.

You might turn heads with external beauty, but you will only turn hearts and change lives by an inner loveliness. Some of the most physically beautiful women I have ever observed were the ugliest due to selfish desires, uncontrolled emotions, and prickly hearts. By contrast, other women who might consider themselves plain or even nondescript, are strikingly beautiful to those who see them by virtue of their inner calm and grace.

⧗   *List three character traits you would like to rid yourself of:*

1. _____

2. _____

3. _____

⧗   *Now, list three character traits you would love to acquire:*

1. _____

2. _____

3. _____

THE MIRROR

⧗ *When you get to the end of your life, how do you hope your family remembers you? The emotional choices you are making today will leave a long and lasting legacy.*

ETERNAL WORDS

Your adornment must not be merely external—braiding the hair, and wearing gold jewelry, or putting on dresses; but let it be the hidden person of the heart, with the imperishable quality of a gentle and quiet spirit, which is precious in the sight of God. (1 Peter 3:3–4)

MY PRAYER FOR TODAY

Jesus, this topic of submission is challenging for me. I pray most of all, I would have the desire to be more like You in all of life's situations. I want to serve like You served and to love like You loved. In Jesus' name I pray. Amen.

Day 5

A Gentle and Quiet Spirit

Are you married? Even if you are single, read on, because I believe you will understand the concept of what I'd like to teach in this lesson.

Do you remember your wedding day? Do you remember how every ounce of energy was invested into creating an absolutely gorgeous bride? I remember shopping for my wedding dress with my mom, my beloved aunt, and my sweet cousin Joy. We scoured bridal shops across the city until we found the perfect dress. I spent hours debating whether I should wear blue or brown eye shadow on my wedding day. If you are a more modern bride, you likely had your hair and nails done for this once-in-a-lifetime occasion.

And then, as I walked down the aisle on my father's trembling arm, my heart stopped when I saw Craig standing by the altar. It seemed as if all my dreams had come true on July 31, 1977, in that little Methodist church in my hometown.

Wives, let's fast forward to today and allow me to pose just a few questions.

Do you weigh the same as you did on your wedding day?

Is your hair the same color it was all those years ago?

Is your skin still youthful and dewy without wrinkles or age spots?

What happened to that Princess Bride you created explicitly for your wedding day?

I hope what has lasted, or perhaps grown even more lovely with time, is your gentle and quiet spirit. A peaceful and humble spirit will never go out of style, it will never age, and it rarely wrinkles. A gentle and quiet spirit is, quite simply, imperishable.

The loveliest feature a woman of any age has to offer is not her outward beauty but her inward calm. As your body begins to age, and it will, your spirit can remain eternally youthful and timelessly beautiful.

Hidden Person

Your adornment must not be merely external—braiding the hair, and wearing gold jewelry, or putting on dresses; but let it be the hidden person of the heart, with the imperishable quality of a gentle and quiet spirit, which is precious in the sight of God. For in this way in former times the holy women also, who hoped in God, used to adorn themselves, being submissive to their own husbands. (1 Peter 3:3–5)

The word for "heart" used in Peter's letter is the Greek word *kardis* which refers to the physical organ of the heart rather than the emotional center of the body. Your heart might stay hidden from view, but it is the most life-giving organ in your magnificent body. Your heart has a direct impact on every single cell in your physical being. Your body is unable to live without your heart.

If the heart is diseased, the body will likely die. If the heart pumps impure or weak blood, the body cannot retain its health. So it is with your spirit. Although your spirit is hidden from the naked eye, it yields vital and life-giving importance to your magnificent life. If you have allowed darkness to inundate your spirit, then your spirit will pump darkness to other areas of your life. However, if your spirit is filled with the nutrition of Scripture and the energy of worship, then your spirit will pump God's life into every single part of your being.

A woman who longs to be the most amazing version of herself possible will invest time and discipline into her spirit, even after her body begins to age.

⧖ *What are you doing to invest time and discipline into your spirit?*

GQ

When a woman cultivates and maintains a gentle and quiet spirit, she is furnishing herself with the gift of ageless appeal. Your spirit will never grow old, nor will it experience the effects of aging when it is gentle and quiet. Peter says this type of spirit is imperishable.

The word *imperishable* means "something that is incapable of decay; something that is incapable of suffering the effects of the wear and tear of aging." A gentle and quiet spirit is forever young.

As I studied the various meanings of the phrase *"gentle and quiet spirit,"* I decided to write my own definition based upon the different facets of its intent.

> *A gentle and quiet spirit has a heart attitude of sweet friendliness, warm friendship, and durable patience. A woman who has fostered these lovely spiritual attributes is known for her enthusiastic kindness and unflappable tenderness.*
>
> *A woman who has cultivated a gentle and quiet spirit does not take advantage of the opportunity to become angry. She refuses anger and even diffuses it with a careful, measured approach to conflict. This amazing woman is quick to forgive and forbids herself to utter words she will later regret.*
>
> *A woman with a gentle and quiet spirit knows the eternal value of responding rather than reacting. She has deliberately decided not to contribute to conflicts but maintains a state of peaceful forbearance and gracious tranquility.*

Although this is an extended definition, I believe you now understand the importance of becoming this woman.

Wives, sisters, daughters, and mothers are afforded numerous opportunities to feel deeply shaken by the events of life or to be perturbed by the affairs of people. But a woman with a quiet and gentle spirit never reverts to worry, whining, or emotional sewage. This woman grips unmatched emotional and spiritual strength. She doesn't verbally vomit on the people who offend her, nor does she burp her opinions in their airspace. She possesses an uncommon strength that enables her to consistently steady the ship and ushers in peace that passes understanding. This gentle and quiet spirit is precious to the Lord—a valuable component in His kingdom.

God knew women would need these attributes to display His character in the workplace, in personal relationships, and in the home. Your quiet and gentle spirit reflects the time you spend with Him. God considers a gentle and quiet spirit rare, precious, and dear.

⧖ *Who do you know that has cultivated a gentle and quiet spirit?*

⧖ *List three possible ways you could encourage a gentle and quiet sprit in your own life:*

1. _____

2. _____

3. _____

And Finally . . . Hope

> *For in this way in former times the holy women also, who hoped in God, used to adorn themselves, being submissive to their own husbands.* (1 Peter 3:5)

If you hope—hope in God. If you trust anyone—trust God. My friend, you don't possess the power to change your husband, whether he is a great man of God or an atheist. Only God is able to change a man, so place all your hope and trust in the One who passionately loves your husband even more than you.

Your hope should remain steadfastly anchored to the Lord—not to your appearance or your power of persuasion. God will have the last word in your marriage and in your husband's heart. Can you trust Him with that?

One Measly Little Verse

Peter spends six times longer focusing on women than on men. Men, or husbands, only get one measly little verse–but what a verse it is.

> *In the same way you married men should live considerately with [your wives], with an intelligent recognition [of the marriage relation], honoring the woman as [physically] the weaker, but [realizing that you] are joint heirs of the grace [God's unmerited favor] of life, in order that your prayers may not be hindered and cut off. [Otherwise you cannot pray effectively].* (1 Peter 3:7 AMPC)

The most accurate translation introducing this verse offers these specific words, *"You husbands, in turn, must know how to live with a woman."*

Perhaps a follow-up question most men might ask is, "Well, how in the world do you do *that?*" Women, most of us are guilty as charged. We have made it extremely difficult for men to solve this mystery. As you have probably surmised, I do have some advice in this area.

First, my friends, be easy to love. You don't have to snap at your husband, regardless of what day of the month it might be. As you travel down this sometimes rocky, always interesting, road of marriage, resolve to be an encourager not a discourager.

Peter refers to women as "the weaker" vessel in the verse aimed at men in the home. Many women wrestle with this concept but I love the phrase Peter used to describe females. The word translated as "weaker" can also mean "more delicate" or "fragile because of its beauty, which makes it more valuable." Peter's profound point is that men should treat their wives with the care befitting a delicate, valuable, and stunning treasure.

My mother, who is a lover of all things beautiful and expensive, owns several sets of English bone china. The rose-covered family heirlooms are proudly displayed in her antique hutch. I, on the other hand, have purchased most of my dishes at either a discount or grocery store when they were running a special. My dishes are durable and family friendly. I treat my mother's dishes much differently than I do my own. Her dishes are delicate and expensive. You, as a woman, are infinitely more valuable than my mother's dishes and should be treated as such.

⧖   *How do you feel about the phrase weaker vessel now that you are aware of its further implications?*

Fellow Heirs

You husbands in the same way, live with your wives in an understanding way, as with someone weaker, since she is a woman; and show her honor as a fellow heir of the grace of life, so that your prayers will not be hindered. (1 Peter 3:7)

The startling reality for a husband is if he does not treat his wife as a beloved treasure, his prayer life will be hindered. And guess what? We are fellow heirs of grace and likely this concept applies to the wife's treatment of her husband as well.

THE MIRROR

⧗ *Do you believe a gentle and quiet spirit has more to do with tempera-ment and personality than it does with your spiritual walk in Christ? Why or why not?*

ETERNAL WORDS

Your adornment must not be merely external—braiding the hair, and wearing gold jewelry, or putting on dresses; but let it be the hidden person of the heart, with the imperishable quality of a gentle and quiet spirit, which is precious in the sight of God. **(1 Peter 3:3–4)**

MY PRAYER FOR TODAY

Jesus, today I place my hope and trust in You. I deeply long to honor You in my human relationships: in my home, the church, and in the workplace. Father, would You work a gentle and quiet spirit into my life? In Jesus' name I pray. Amen.

Week 7

Living the Life

Day 1

Life Prep

Peter became an expert in preparing people for the journey of life and in producing healthy human relationships. He is the New Testament expert on both topics. Peter's choice to love and know Jesus changed his nature from impetuous and emotional to responsive and stable. The Holy Spirit had accomplished a refining work in Peter's personality. No longer was he blustery, domineering, and belligerent; he became a vibrant show-and-tell reflecting the character of Jesus Christ.

⧗ *What has the Lord changed in you since you became a Christian?*

Summing It Up

If you are wondering how to treat someone with whom you are in relationship, Peter presents character traits of timeless and Christlike impact in the following section of Scripture.

> **To sum up, all of you be harmonious, sympathetic, brotherly, kind-hearted, and humble in spirit. (1 Peter 3:8)**

This verse is among the most wonderfully practical in Peter's entire discourse. He presents a relationship "to-do" list for those who are known as Christians. His expectation is that we would take to heart his resounding advice. Here is Peter's list:

- **Harmonious**—As believers in Christ, we don't all have to play the exact same note, but we all must sing in the same key. Our lives are to stay concordant with one another as our differences blend to create something of soaring beauty rather than harsh dissonance.

- **Sympathetic**—This word means "to suffer together or to feel someone's pain." I can be extraordinarily sympathetic with those I love, but when it is someone with whom I disagree or who has been unkind to me, I have found it difficult to feel sympathetic. I deeply desire to be sympathetic with everyone and to feel their unique pain. Sympathetic can also be translated as *compassionate*. Compassion is nearly a lost virtue because of what we expose ourselves to on the nightly news and in the entertainment world. We view starving children daily, repeatedly hear about deaths in cities and schools, and see the devastation of war and cruelty. This has hardened our hearts to the common life pains of others. I have often prayed the prayer of Bob Pierce, "Let my heart be broken with the things that break the heart of God."

- **Brotherly**—Peter is calling us to a lifestyle of affectionate friendship or deep love for those around us. Everyone we meet needs a kind brother or sister.

- **Kindhearted**—Kindness is not just a feeling; it always produces action. Dormant kindness is nonexistent. Kindness will move you to change someone's situation by whatever means necessary. Kindness is vital in family relationships, in the neighborhood, in church, and at your workplace. Kindness diffuses anger, erases bitterness, and ushers in sweet peace. God's will for your life is to be the kindest person possible during your tenure on planet earth—and with God, all things *are* possible.

- **Humble in spirit**—This three-word phrase is a reminder not to be a know-it-all, but to listen, and then offer a voice of encouragement. Remove all judgmental tendencies from your temperament and resolve to always say, "Let me help you with that."

⧖ *Which one of the above character traits is the most challenging for you?*

⌛ *Which one is easily a part of who you are as a person?*

Stop It

Every mother knows when her children are disobedient one too many times, the words "Stop it. Just stop it. That's enough!" can effectively bring errant behavior to an end.

> ***Not returning evil for evil or insult for insult, but giving a blessing instead; for you were called for the very purpose that you might inherit a blessing.* (1 Peter 3:9)**

This verse carries a much stronger tone than you might believe by reading its relatively benign verbiage. However, Peter's intent and word usage is imperative rather than gentle and instructive in nature.

Peter targeted retaliation in a believer's heart and demanded the Body of Christ be done with counterattack. It takes two people to fight, and a Christian should never enter a war of words. Offering mercy and forgiveness provides a more potent posture than being a person of bitterness and revenge. The Bible never states that we are allowed to treat people in the same manner they have treated us. The Word of God is unremitting in the inerrant truth of fully pardoning and then blessing those who have wronged us—regardless of what instinct says.

A child's first impulse is to strike back at the person who threw the first punch, but you, my sister, are not a child. Adults often do their hitting back in more sophisticated and acceptable ways. We give our husbands the silent treatment, gossip about a coworker, wear the martyr syndrome as a badge of honor, or withdraw from relationships. God wants you to inherit a life of blessing and the way you do that is by offering an undeserved blessing to offenders.

When your flesh and emotions are riled due to mistreatment or rejection, run to the Lord, and ask Him to help you perceive this situation from His perspective. If you allow the Holy Spirit to work in your heart, He will show you how to respond in kindness despite the offense. Resolve to become an unoffendable woman who is determined to not only *give* a blessing but to *be* a blessing.

Peter was not the only New Testament author who encouraged this type of consecrated and godly behavior. Take the time to read the following verses and linger over each one. Ask the Holy Spirit to help you demonstrate this sterling conduct.

> *Bless those who persecute you; bless and do not curse.* **(Romans 12:14)**

> *Never pay back evil for evil to anyone.* **(Romans 12:17)**

> *And we toil, working with our own hands, when we are reviled, we bless; when we are persecuted, we endure.* **(1 Corinthians 4:12)**

> *See that no one repays another with evil for evil, but always seek after that which is good for one another and for all people.* **(1 Thessalonians 5:15)**

Would you read those four verses above one more time? As you prayerfully re-read this timeless input, become the woman you have always wanted to be and adopt this lifestyle as your very own.

⧗ *Isn't it wonderful not to remain in bondage to human emotions or fractious people? Isn't it wonderful to be set free to live like Jesus?*

⧗ *Is there anyone in your life to whom you have demonstrated bitterness or anger? How can you bless this person today in Jesus' name?*

Retaliate

Let me assure you that certain people and situations do call for an instant retaliation—however, you might be surprised at the type of retaliation to which I am referring.

> *Do not repay wrong with wrong, or abuse with abuse; on the contrary, retaliate with blessing, for a blessing is the inheritance to which you yourselves have been called.* (1 Peter 3:9 NEB)

When you simply must retaliate and are unable to restrain yourself–retaliate with a blessing. It's a radical response. It's timeless. And it works!

THE MIRROR

⧗ *Did you feel corrected or encouraged today by the Holy Spirit? I believe difficult relationships reveal what is in our hearts more than most any other situation can. Does your heart need cleansing toward a certain person? Ask the Lord to give you creative ideas on how to "retaliate with a blessing" toward that person and then list them below.*

1. _____

2. _____

3. _____

ETERNAL WORDS

To sum up, all of you be harmonious, sympathetic, brotherly, kind-hearted, and humble in spirit; not returning evil for evil or insult for insult, but giving a blessing instead; for you were called for the very purpose that you might inherit a blessing. (1 Peter 3:8–9)

MY PRAYER FOR TODAY

Jesus, I want to be a retaliator. I want to always retaliate with a blessing. Give me creative ideas of how I can bless the most difficult person in my life. In Jesus' name I pray. Amen.

Day 2

Loving the Life You Have Been Given

I love life! I love everything about it. I love all the possibilities it proposes throughout the hallways of time.

I love spending time with the people I love the most and know the best.

I love working in the warm soil of the garden in springtime as I anticipate the rainbow of flowers that will soon burst their little heads into the warmth of the sunshine.

I love the steam that rises over the cup of a hot chocolate on a January day as I sit in front of my fireplace with a book that's called my name.

I love going for a brisk walk through the rustle of autumn leaves, breathing deeply of the chilly air that clears my mind and rejuvenates my soul.

I love holding a baby. Nuzzling its little neck. And smelling its breath so fresh from heaven.

But how do you feel about life and the capacity to love after tragedy has impaled your heart?

Admittedly, I have survived some very dark days, but even in the abyss, I have always discovered something to express gratitude for and found a reason to hope again. Peter can relate. He is writing to a scattered, battered, and persecuted church. And yet he exhibits the boldness to encourage these emotionally bruised and spiritually rejected people. If you read between the lines of this next passage, perhaps you will discern, as I did, Peter's intent to remind this sterling yet pummeled people how to continue loving the life you are living even when fraught with enormous pain.

A Wonderful Life in the Fire

The following three verses quote Psalm 34:12–16. How wonderful to know that as Peter writes to the broken church, he is reciting the words of King David, a man after God's own heart.

For,

> *"The one who desires life, to love and see good days,*
>
> *Must keep his tongue from evil and his lips from speaking deceit.*
>
> *He must turn away from evil and do good;*
>
> *He must seek peace and pursue it.*
>
> *For the eyes of the Lord are toward the righteous,*
>
> *And His ears attend to their prayer,*
>
> *But the face of the Lord is against those who do evil."* (1 Peter 3:10–12)

There is still a way to enjoy a fulfilling and even thrilling life in the middle of messy politics, ill-treatment, and threat of death. If your desire is to love life and see good days, there are several practical components you can layer into the horror that might currently surround you.

It might sound ridiculous and even lackluster, but Peter coaches these broken people to first *"keep your tongue from evil and your lips from speaking deceit."*

The word *keep* in this compound phrase literally means to pause. The meaning indicates that before you speak an unkind or cruel word, it is wise to strategically pause. Daily, according to Peter, we should we hit the pause button located in our souls before we are tempted to lie or exaggerate. If you want to live the abundant life Christ died on the cross to give you, then you must refrain from uttering destructive words against another person made in the image of Christ. If you long to bask in the pleasure of a long and happy life, it is imperative to take a break from destroying someone with your tongue. Your lips were not created to speak guile, trickery, or manipulation; instead, you were given lips for the purpose of praising the Lord and encouraging others.

My friend, refuse to live in the garbage dump of emotional justification but bring yourself up higher into God's presence where there is always fullness of joy. If you desire to live a wonderful life despite the state of the world and regardless of the status of your personal life, what you communicate casts the deciding vote. Your tongue determines what road you will travel upon as well as frames the atmosphere of your days.

Once you press pause on verbal vomit, you must then resolve to live a life of righteousness and peace. You must intentionally and consistently do deeds of goodness and kindness for others whose lives have intersected with your own.

⧗   *Why do you believe such a small thing as controlling your tongue is able to repurpose the type of life you are living?*

Be a Zealot

When I have a difficult decision to make, I often silently quote this phrase to myself, *Seek peace and pursue it.*

In today's biblical passage, the Greek word Peter utilizes for *seek* is the intense word *zeteo.* The English word *zealot* is derived from *zeteo,* which means "to earnestly seek, to passionately go after, to earnestly inquire." When you *zeteo* an object, a person, or a lifestyle, you crave it with your whole heart. There is nothing flimsy or lackadaisical about a person who *zeteos* peace, but this person is so determined to embrace peace that nothing will move her and no one will distract her.

Seeking peace, therefore, is not passive but is meant to be an active part of your life. I have discovered there is a decided difference between peacekeepers and peacemakers.

- A peacekeeper wants peace at any cost, including at the exclusion of standing up for what is right and honorable. Peacekeepers refuse to state a controversial opinion even when it is scripturally based. They fly the white flag of surrender so no one will be in opposition to their stand. A peacekeeper is often more concerned with pleasing people than she is determined to please the Lord. While peacekeepers do guard the peace that already exists, they refuse to take any more real estate for the great cause of peace.

- A peacemaker, on the other hand, is willing to fight for peace. They understand they have the power and authority of Scripture on their side, so they state God's principles in a loving but definitive manner. Peacemakers will never compromise God's truth but will boldly pursue righteousness until it rules and reigns.

If you are deeply yearning to embrace the life of your dreams, you will seek peace and pursue it. Perhaps this list of practical disciplines will facilitate your enthusiastic quest for peace:

- Don't be a troublemaker with a bent toward gossip.
- Speak in gentle tones and with tender words.
- Take your anxious thoughts captive with a scripture verse.
- Whenever you are afraid or worried, choose to trust the Lord instead.
- Find a Bible verse that will fight your battles for you.
- Listen to worship music to calm your anxious soul.
- Serve others who have been unkind to you.
- Smile sincerely and be generous.

⧗ *Are you a peacemaker or a peacekeeper? State the reason why.*

The Eyes of the Lord

FOR THE EYES OF THE LORD ARE TOWARD THE RIGHTEOUS,

AND HIS EARS ATTEND TO THEIR PRAYER,

BUT THE FACE OF THE LORD IS AGAINST THOSE WHO DO EVIL. **(1 Peter 3:12)**

The emphatic reason your life will be enjoyable and filled with timeless peace is because the Lord will watch you every hour of every day. The choices you make, how you treat others, and the disciplines you incorporate into your life captivate Him. Not only are the Lord's eyes upon your life but so are His ears. His ears are listening intently to every prayer you pray, every verse you declare, and every song you sing.

THE MIRROR

Do you have any regrets in life? If so, what are they in a general sense? As a believer in Christ, how can you handle your regrets in a God-honoring manner?

ETERNAL WORDS

To sum up, all of you be harmonious, sympathetic, brotherly, kind-hearted, and humble in spirit; not returning evil for evil or insult for insult, but giving a blessing instead; for you were called for the very purpose that you might inherit a blessing. (1 Peter 3:8–9)

MY PRAYER FOR TODAY

Lord Jesus, I deeply desire to live a glorious life that only honors You. Help me to control my mouth and to be a zealot for peace in all my relationships. Father, thank You for watching me and for listening to me. In Jesus' name I pray. Amen.

Day 3

The Invitation of Suffering

My greatest delight in life is teaching timeless principles found in the Word of God to women. I especially enjoy it when those principles are focused upon blessings, favor, and the loving kindness of the Father. However, to embrace a complete view of Scripture, there are times when we must humbly listen to the Lord's plan for those who are suffering. We will all suffer at some moment in our lives, and we must be prepared to suffer well and even joyfully. It's vital to have a God-honoring theology on the topic of suffering rather than blissfully ignoring it. Hoping suffering won't knock on the door of our hearts is futile–because it will. It surely will.

⧗ *What is your definition of the word suffering?*

⧗ *Based upon your definition, have you ever suffered?*

An Invitation

As we begin to intensely gaze at the topic of suffering, allow me to remind you that the Bible promises this:

> **What then shall we say to these things? If God is for us, who is against us? (Romans 8:31)**

God will never leave or forsake you when your life has gone up in smoke or when you are tormented for righteousness' sake. The Holy Spirit made this promise to the early church and it is your promise today as well.

Over the course of my life, I have found times of undeserved and cruel suffering often come with invitations. How you respond to these divine invitations is up to you.

> *Who is there to harm you if you prove zealous for what is good? But even if you should suffer for the sake of righteousness, you are blessed. AND DO NOT FEAR THEIR INTIMIDATION, AND DO NOT BE TROUBLED. (1 Peter 3:13–14)*

Peter's sacred summons in the middle of human suffering is to look for the blessing in it.

- When men revile believers—God blesses them.
- When people mock—the Lord blesses.
- When friends walk away—God stays.
- When family members ridicule—God blesses His dearly loved children.

One of the sterling lessons discovered in the invitation of suffering is not to be dependent upon the blessing of people but upon the blessing of the Father. Remember this New Testament promise, my friend, when you suffer for the sake of righteousness: God always responds with a blessing. It is a privilege to suffer for the cause of Jesus Christ. It is a high honor to count yourself among the ranks of Esther, Peter, Paul, Daniel, Stephen, and others.

⧖ *If you have ever suffered, what blessing did you discover in the middle of the agony?*

The Second Invitation

> *But sanctify Christ as Lord in your hearts, always being ready to make a defense to everyone who asks you to give an account for the hope that is in you, yet with gentleness and reverence.* (1 **Peter 3:15**)

Peter invites the persecuted Body of Christ to intently focus on giving the Lord a high and holy place in their hearts during dreadful days. Through my painful periods, I learned to remain more aware of Christ's presence than of my persecutors or the devil. I set my heart upon the Lord in worship and in adoration.

Peter also paints a picture of using a period of suffering as a vivid and exciting time of evangelism. In the middle of a storm that has ravaged your life, ask the Lord to give you an opportunity to share the gospel with someone in pain.

> *Jesus, send someone my way today who needs to know about Your love and forgiveness.*

As you share your vibrant faith, make sure you do so with gentle words and honor. When tragedy assails and as storm clouds gather, people should not see you panic but they should be mesmerized by your indefatigable hope.

Many believers in Christ are intimidated by the very thought of witnessing and therefore dread opportunities to share their faith. If you are one of the believers I just described, you need to place yourself in God's line for a heart transplant. There is a world going to hell and we have the answers and hope for which they desperately long. Have you considered the possibility that you just might lead someone to the Lord?

My friend, it is impossible to be an undercover Christian, especially during times of anguish. Simply think of evangelism as allowing Jesus to leak out of you. The testimony of your life was meant to make it easier for someone else to believe in God.

⧖   *Do you dread witnessing? Why or why not?*

⧖   *Think of someone you feel called to share your testimony with. Now, write three to four sentences about how you could begin this conversation.*

Your Conscience Is Your Friend

Do you recall the familiar children's song performed enthusiastically by a little cricket who playfully but sincerely bids the listener to always be guided by one's conscience? Jiminy Cricket's reminder is a wise one and even Scripture backs it up.

Peter invited his dearly loved brothers and sisters in Christ to stand poignantly and constantly in tune with their conscience.

> **And keep a good conscience so that in the thing in which you are slandered, those who revile your good behavior in Christ will be put to shame. (1 Peter 3:16)**

This advice roars through the ages—we simply must not ignore the injunction to keep a good conscience in everything we undertake. How vital it is to keep our personal integrity before God and to ensure we never make a choice that will usher in shame later.

Conscience is simply the ability to distinguish between that which is morally good and morally bad—we must do the former and shun the latter. As followers of Christ, how important it is to stay conscious of wrongdoing. We must select actions that reflect our relationship with God the Father and Jesus the Son.

THE MIRROR

⧖   *In a practical sense, how do you keep a good conscience? What does that mean exactly?*

ETERNAL WORDS

To sum up, all of you be harmonious, sympathetic, brotherly, kind-hearted, and humble in spirit; not returning evil for evil or insult for insult, but giving a blessing instead; for you were called for the very purpose that you might inherit a blessing. (1 Peter 3:8–9)

MY PRAYER FOR TODAY

Father God, would You give me divine appointments this very day to share my faith? Give me the boldness of Peter as I tell others about Your goodness and forgiveness. And Father, help me to live an unashamed life that honors You. In Jesus' name I pray. Amen.

Day 4

A Huge Question

Are you ready to wrestle? It's time for us to grapple with suffering so we can discover what God's will is during times of trauma, intense emotional pain, and ravaging physical agony.

The mystery of suffering has plagued believers nearly from the beginning of time. Consider the following:

- the murder of Abel by Cain
- Earth's utter destruction caused by the great flood
- Job's unimaginable torment
- Egyptian bondage for the children of Israel
- Saul's relentless pursuit of David
- the three Hebrew boys thrown into the fiery furnace
- Daniel tossed into the lions' den
- Paul and Silas unfairly imprisoned
- the persecution of the early church

Have you ever seen such an extensive list of affliction? The accounts of suffering in the Bible are nearly too numerous to mention. Suffering is indeed a mystery, and we must trust our good, good Father with that mystery.

⧖ *What do you dread the most about the possibility of suffering in the days to come?*

⏳ *Can you think of a scripture verse that could help you during dif-ficult days?*

God's Will

> *For it is better, if God should will it so, that you suffer for doing what is right rather than for doing what is wrong. For Christ also died for sins once for all, the just for the unjust, so that He might bring us to God, having been put to death in the flesh, but made alive in the spirit.* (1 Peter 3:17–18)

The first concept we need to contend with is this, *What is the will of God?* God's will, simply stated, is His inclination, His desire, and His pleasure.

God's purpose, as you and I have already experienced, is to bless mankind through the arrival, death, and resurrection of Jesus Christ. We should never ignore the compelling truth that Christ had to suffer so we could be forgiven and spend eternity in heaven.

You will have to persist in the struggle, as I have, to discern God's will in the mystery of suffering. I have grappled with this enigma nearly my entire adult life through my experiences. I find comfort by reading views of great theologians, by asking men and women who are much wiser than I what their views are, and of course, by spending time in the matchless Word of God.

I do not believe God *wills* or *desires* suffering for His beloved children. He does not wish us to experience pain, nor does He send it. It is not His inclination to make us hurt during our human walk. However, since we live in a broken, fallen, sinful world, suffering is indeed part of the human condition. In our pain, we share in the sufferings of Jesus Christ which is a glorious calling for us.

> *But to the degree that you share the sufferings of Christ, keep on rejoic-ing, so that also at the revelation of His glory you may rejoice with exultation.* (1 Peter 4:13)

My friend, at all times, choose to exhibit a Christlike behavior in humility, honoring others, showing kindness to those around you, and looking for opportunities to lead others to His amazing grace.

⧗   *In a practical sense, make a list of actions you can exhibit if you do suffer.*

1. _____

2. _____

3. _____

Do It Right

> *For it is better, if God should will it so, that you suffer for doing what is right rather than for doing what is wrong. For Christ also died for sins once for all, the just for the unjust, so that He might bring us to God, having been put to death in the flesh, but made alive in the spirit.* **(1 Peter 3:17–18)**

As we read Peter's words to the early church, he states that God's will is for suffering to only come upon the Body of Christ because of doing what is right. There is a suffering that follows wrongdoing, but the Lord does not hope for that type of suffering to be part of your human experience.

Suffering often does come from sin, doesn't it? Having sex outside of marriage can result in all types of consequences, such as disease, broken marriages, and unplanned pregnancies. However, allow me to also quickly say that a baby is not *the* suffering that follows. Babies are always a blessing regardless of how they arrive. But the unwed mother and father must face the results created from their choice.

Certain diseases, not all, but some, do invade our bodies resulting from sinful choices such as overeating, smoking, or addictions to alcohol and drugs.

Car accidents happen when people drink too much or break the law by speeding, texting, or through other driving infractions.

If you cheat on your taxes, which is sin, you will have to deal with the punishment thereof.

> *Make sure that none of you suffers as a murderer, or thief, or evildoer, or a troublesome meddler.* **(1 Peter 4:15)**

⧗   *Have you ever suffered because of your own sinful choices?*

⧗   *Have you ever suffered due to someone else's sinful choices?*

⧗   *How were these two experiences different?*

Sowing and Reaping

Suffering is often the logical consequence of sin. It is known as cause and effect or sowing and reaping.

> **Do not be deceived, God is not mocked; for whatever a man sows, this he will also reap. For the one who sows to his own flesh will from the flesh reap corruption, but the one who sows to the Spirit will from the Spirit reap eternal life. (Galatians 6:7–8)**

It's as simple as realizing if you place your hand on a hot object you will get burned. As I listen to the heartache of women daily through prayer requests and e-mails, I am aware of a very sad fact: *many Christians suffer in a specific area of life due to disobedience to the Lord and to His Word.*

If you are in a season of financial hardship, I must ask you, *Are you consistently tithing?*

If you are dealing with a difficult person, may I gently ask, *Are you loving your enemy in word and deed? Are you blessing those who curse you? Are you walking in uncommon forgiveness?*

If you are suffering because of disobedience to the Word of God, there is a glorious and freeing solution—immediately repent and ask for forgiveness. Ask for the power of the Holy Spirit to invade your life so you will have the discipline and strength to live for Jesus daily. Read the Word of God, just soak it up in your soul and it will change the desires of your heart.

> *How can a young man keep his way pure?*
> *By keeping it according to Your word.* **(Psalm 119:9)**

There Is a Blessing

Suffering in the life of a believer can also come from doing the right thing. If you choose to read your Bible publicly at work or school, others may mock you. If you choose not to serve alcohol at a celebratory event, your family may be offended and refuse to attend. If you make a habit of attending church rather than sporting events or social gatherings, people in your life may feel frustrated with your choice. If you don't participate in gossip or laugh at off-color jokes, you might be known as a "goody two-shoes" or "holier than thou." If you are consistently kind to a person whom everyone else shuns or mocks, you will be misunderstood. But suffering for doing the righteous thing is worth it. Let's look at what Jesus says.

> *Blessed are you when people insult you and persecute you, and falsely say all kinds of evil against you because of Me. Rejoice and be glad, for your reward in heaven is great; for in the same way they persecuted the prophets who were before you.* **(Matthew 5:11–12)**

If you suffer for doing the right thing, you are in good company with Paul and Silas, Peter, Daniel, Noah, and Jesus. Carry on, precious sister in the Lord. Ask God to give you the strength and tenacity to honor Him in all your ways.

THE MIRROR

⧗ *Life is hard at times, isn't it? What are some of the disciplines you can incorporate into your own life to ensure that in the face of suffering, you will have the strength equal to the task?*

1. _____

2. _____

3. _____

ETERNAL WORDS

To sum up, all of you be harmonious, sympathetic, brotherly, kind-hearted, and humble in spirit; not returning evil for evil or insult for insult, but giving a blessing instead; for you were called for the very purpose that you might inherit a blessing. (1 Peter 3:8–9)

MY PRAYER FOR TODAY

Dear Jesus, I certainly don't want to suffer, but if I do, thank You for the promise that You will never leave me or forsake me. Thank You for the power of Your Holy Spirit and for the wisdom in Your Word. In Jesus' name I pray. Amen.

Day 5

Absolutely Free!

Our daughter, Joni, had just returned from India after spending nearly a year working at a girls' home in that poverty-stricken land. She needed a car as she was starting a job in a distant city while working on her master's degree. Craig happened to mention her need early one morning when he was in a prayer group with some of his friends. One of the men said, "Well, I have my mother-in-law's old car. I'll fix it up for her and give it to her."

Of course, we were overwhelmed by his generosity and knew Joni would feel grateful for this used car the man guaranteed to be in excellent condition.

The day Joni flew home, this incredible friend asked us to take her straight from the airport to a car dealership. We wondered what his mother-in-law's old car was doing at the dealership, but we didn't ask any questions.

As we walked in the front door, everyone who worked there smiled and seemed so excited about something we apparently were not privy to. They ushered us to a back room filled with purple balloons and there stood our friend with another woman from our church. They had bought Joni a brand-new car, a top-of-the-line model. A coffee mug that matched the vehicle waited inside it, as well as an envelope filled with cash to cover Joni's taxes on the car.

We were all weeping, and so was everyone else in the dealership. The gift seemed too generous, too extravagant to be true. We were overwhelmed with deep gratitude. I will never forget that day.

Has anyone ever given you a gift so outrageously undeserved and bountiful? If you answered no, think again. Someone has given you a lavish gift—His name is Jesus.

The Entire Amount

> *For Christ also died for sins once for all, the just for the unjust, so that He might bring us to God, having been put to death in the flesh, but made alive in the spirit.* (1 Peter 3:18)

I love the three-word phrase hidden among the magnificence of this verse: *once for all*. Christ paid the entire amount for your salvation, and you don't owe a dime! You will never be charged for this extravagant and undeserved grace Christ has given you. Your sin bill is paid in full and you will never owe anything *ever again*.

I have never understood the concept I am about to share with you; however, I assure you it is an eternal and timeless truth. When you accepted the forgiveness of Jesus Christ, not only were your past sins forgiven, but your future sins were forgiven as well.

He was the just and we were the unjust. In the Greek, the word for "just" is singular while the word for "unjust" is plural. There is only one of Him—only one just. There are millions of unjust and yet the One paid for the millions. He did it all.

Although Jesus was cruelly crucified on the cross of Calvary, His Spirit is now alive forevermore. An exciting and nearly unbelievable aspect of the gift you have received is that you were formerly dead in your sins but now your spirit is alive forevermore.

You and I will continue to be like Christ in this wonderful truth—our flesh will die but our spirits will never perish because of the price He paid. Your spirit is now timeless and will never experience death.

⧗ *What are some of your benefits due to the promise that you are now "alive in the spirit"?*

1. _____

2. _____

3. _____

Not This

There are passages and concepts in the Bible difficult to understand without the advantage of seminary or intense biblical study. The following verses have always challenged my mind and spirit as I struggle to understand what the Holy Spirit endeavors to communicate. When principles are difficult to comprehend and when the theology seems murky, we must not shy away from digging for at least one nugget of eternal gold in a passage. So, let's excavate and ask the Holy Spirit to give us insight:

In which also He went and made proclamation to the spirits now in prison, who once were disobedient, when the patience of God kept waiting in the days of Noah, during the construction of the ark, in which a few, that is, eight persons, were brought safely through the water. (1 Peter 3:19–20)

There are spirits now suffering in an eternal prison due to their disobedience and lack of repentance. They rejected God and His ways. These lost spirits will never be free from the prison their own choices led them into. My heart is ravaged as I consider these people and the singular decisions that resulted in eternal suffering. I long to lead just one person away from this horrific fate. I pray the timeless impact of my life will mean hell is smaller and heaven is bigger because I told others about Jesus.

⧖ *We've talked about this before, but we must cover it again. Who in your world needs to know the saving power of Jesus Christ?*

1. _____

2. _____

3. _____

Pause and pray right now that the Lord will use you in leading this person away from sin and into forgiveness.

Those who embrace Christ will experience eternal blessing and abundant life because we have entered the ark of His presence and forgiveness.

Corresponding to that, baptism now saves you—not the removal of dirt from the flesh, but an appeal to God for a good conscience—through the resurrection of Jesus Christ, who is at the right hand of God, having gone into heaven, after angels and authorities and powers had been subjected to Him. (1 Peter 3:21–22)

Baptism is the symbolic act demonstrating salvation is accomplished in the life of a believer. Baptism is more than just a spiritual bath. It is a holy seal or a sacrament that publicly declares, "I am saved. I am forgiven. I belong to the resurrected Christ."

After salvation, when a believer decides to be baptized, the proclamations heard through this one symbolic act include:

- *Yes, Lord! I am Yours.*
- *I believe the promise of salvation.*
- *I identify with Your people.*
- *I establish Your leadership in my life.*
- *I now join with a host of saints who love You and trust You.*

I have always wondered if Peter wrote the following words with tears streaming down his weather-beaten cheeks, *Who is at the right hand of God, having gone into heaven, after angels and authorities and powers had been subjected to Him.*

Peter had seen Jesus lifted into heaven as He returned to live eternally with God the Father. Jesus now sits at the right hand of God ever making intercession for those of us who still live in the confines of time. When Jesus returned to the glory of heaven after His resurrection, He left the Holy Spirit to comfort, teach, and to empower. Although Jesus is now out of our human sight, He is never beyond our human experience.

You've Got the Power

God, the Father, gave all the power and authority of heaven to Jesus when He came to planet earth as a baby. Everything on earth and in heaven is subject to Christ. And He shares it with no one—except you!

As a believer in Christ, you have been given the same authority as Jesus. Do you believe it? The Holy Spirit endues believers in every historic moment with the power of heaven. This ability is especially designed to create bold witnesses and courageous evangelists.

> **But you will receive power when the Holy Spirit has come upon you; and you shall be My witnesses both in Jerusalem, and in all Judea and Samaria, and even to the remotest part of the earth. (Acts 1:8)**

We need the power of the Holy Spirit to dwell inside of us so we have the strength to make it through an ordinary or demanding day. I can barely pull myself out of bed in the morning without His power. I am unable to make a righteous decision without the matchless power of the Holy Spirit. I especially need an inner power to deal with my out-of-control emotions.

That He would grant you, according to the riches of His glory, to be strengthened with power through His Spirit in the inner man, so that Christ may dwell in your hearts through faith; and that you, being rooted and grounded in love, may be able to comprehend with all the saints what is the breadth and length and height and depth, and to know the love of Christ which surpasses knowledge, that you may be filled up to all the fullness of God.

Now to Him who is able to do far more abundantly beyond all that we ask or think, according to the power that works within us. **(Ephesians 3:16–20)**

⧗ *What do you need power for today?*

1. _____
2. _____
3. _____

Write a prayer asking the Holy Spirit to give you the power for those challenges.

THE MIRROR

⧗ *If you are a believer in Christ, have you been baptized yet? Why is baptism important for a believer?*

⧗ *What does it mean to you to be filled with the power of the Holy Spirit?*

ETERNAL WORDS

To sum up, all of you be harmonious, sympathetic, brotherly, kind-hearted, and humble in spirit; not returning evil for evil or insult for insult, but giving a blessing instead; for you were called for the very purpose that you might inherit a blessing. (1 Peter 3:8–9)

MY PRAYER FOR TODAY

Dear Jesus, thank You for sending the Holy Spirit to be my Comforter, my Teacher, and my Source of eternal power. Fill me today with the Holy Spirit's ability so I can honor You in all my ways. In Jesus' name I pray. Amen.

Week 8

The Benefit Package

Day 1

It's a Conundrum

What I am about to tell you might seem unbelievable at first. It's a true mental conundrum. But I believe as we study the Word together, you will discover, as I have, that the experience of suffering is not a deficit. In many ways, it can be a benefit.

If you believe Romans 8:28 means exactly what it says, then you will know that often, hidden in the turmoil of suffering, there is a blessing. Our God in His great goodness is able to trump the trauma with an eternal blessing.

> *And we know that God causes all things to work together for good to those who love God, to those who are called according to His purpose.* **(Romans 8:28)**

When you study the above verse on its own, it provides a powerful reminder of the loving authority of the Lord. His goodness will always have the final say. However, if you move to the next verse in this significant chapter of Romans 8, it reveals what the goodness of God may accomplish in our lives.

> *For those whom He foreknew, He also predestined to become conformed to the image of His Son, so that He would be the firstborn among many brethren.* **(Romans 8:29)**

What if one of the blessings that belongs to you because of suffering is that it conforms you to the image of Jesus? What if suffering is used as a divine make-over so you are able to demonstrate the character and love of Christ? What if?

⧗   *Have you experienced any benefits from an experience of suffering?*

The Work of Suffering

Suffering carries the propensity to deal with our flesh issues as nothing else can. When suffering enters our lives, one's flesh either demands its own way and screams in pain, or it dies to self and becomes more like Jesus.

> *Therefore, since Christ has suffered in the flesh, arm yourselves also with the same purpose, because he who has suffered in the flesh has ceased from sin, so as to live the rest of the time in the flesh no longer for the lusts of men, but for the will of God.* **(1 Peter 4:1–2)**

Suffering invites a Christian to live no longer for self but to live miraculously for the will and purposes of God.

A mature Christian is able to die to the flesh and live for God even when there is not suffering involved, but for many of us, dying to the flesh requires suffering. Peter reminds Christians in all epochs of the faith that when suffering is part of the human experience, we cease from sin. Reading the truth in this verse, my instant prayer is, *Oh, Jesus, how I long to cease from sin!*

However, perhaps an even more powerful prayer might be, *Jesus, I want to be finished with sin—before I go through an experience of suffering.*

⧗ *What does it mean to "die to the flesh"?*

⧗ *Is it possible for a human to totally "cease from sin"?*

Move On

We all wrestle with a sin nature common to the human condition. When we come to Christ and are adopted into the family of God, although we are still made of flesh, we now have the power to overcome sin and negate it from our character. The bold Peter was well acquainted with a sin nature, but not afraid to confront it intentionally and assertively as he taught the early church to live triumphantly for Christ.

> *For the time already past is sufficient for you to have carried out the desire of the Gentiles, having pursued a course of sensuality, lusts, drunkenness, carousing, drinking parties and abominable idolatries. In all this, they are surprised that you do not run with them into the same excesses of dissipation, and they malign you.* **(1 Peter 4:3–4)**

Peter presented a list of mammoth sins and honestly, I don't relate to most of them. I have never been known as a carouser or dealt with drunkenness or abominable idolatries. I am also quick to admit, however, some sins have targeted my mind and heart for decades. Perhaps you can relate to the sins that knock on the door of my human soul:

- Jealousy and comparison
- Getting my feelings hurt and letting others know
- Demanding my own way
- Wanting more than I can afford
- Being fixated on my past
- Thinking thoughts I should not think
- Saying things I should not say

Peter calls believers away from the distraction of wasting one's life on sin, regardless of what that sin might be. It's time for us to move on from the sin that consistently alienates us from becoming more like Jesus. Life is heartbreakingly short. We must intentionally live our lives for the unshakable kingdom of Christ rather than for our own fleshly desires and weaknesses.

> ⧖ *I was vulnerable with you and shared some of the sin issues that bother me. Would you vulnerably and honestly share your list?*

1. _____

2. _____

3. _____

An Odd Bunch

We Christians are an odd bunch, aren't we? We don't make much sense to the culture in which we live. We don't plunge into every party, and we often go to church while others are at sporting events, shopping online, or even lying in bed. Christians have the reputation of giving away money while the movers and shakers of our generation maximize every investment opportunity. Believers in Jesus Christ pray about matters that normal, levelheaded, reasonable people would instantly take to court in a lawsuit. And we are satisfied with monogamy. How quaint of us.

We don't run with the world and join in their dissipation. Our eyes are on Jesus and our flesh is dying daily. Our priorities have dramatically changed because of salvation and now we find ourselves moving in the opposite direction of the world we live in. What an odd bunch we are.

THE MIRROR

⧗　*Do you believe it is possible to have a close friendship with a nonbeliever and not be impacted by their lifestyle? By their speech? By their preferences?*

⧗　*What is the purpose of a close relationship with someone who does not know Christ?*

ETERNAL WORDS

Above all, keep fervent in your love for one another, because love covers a multitude of sins. Be hospitable to one another without complaint. As each one has received a special gift, employ it in serving one another as good stewards of the manifold grace of God. (1 Peter 4:8–10)

MY PRAYER FOR TODAY

Jesus, hold me close to You. I pray suffering would not be my portion here on earth, but if it is, I thank You that You will be with me and give me the power I need. Jesus, help me to grow daily more like You. In Your name I pray. Amen.

Day 2

All Rise!

Have you ever been summoned to a court of law? Were you ever present when the judge walked into the courtroom dressed in his or her robes? Have you heard the resounding words, "All rise for the judge"? Have you ever watched the magistrate sit down regally in front of the gathered crowd, bang the gavel on the platform, and declare, "Court is now in session"?

The courtroom can be an intimidating, impressive place in which justice is served, punishment is determined, and law is honored. If you have never stood in a courtroom, I can assure you there will come a day when you will stand before the Almighty Judge—your Maker.

Guilty or Innocent

One magnificent day we will all rise for the eternal Judge. At this momentous occasion, our eternal destiny will be revealed.

> *But they will give account to Him who is ready to judge the living and the dead.*
>
> *For the gospel has for this purpose been preached even to those who are dead, that though they are judged in the flesh as men, they may live in the spirit according to the will of God. (1 Peter 4:5–6)*

The guilty sentence will be handed to those who have lived for the flesh and refused the forgiveness of Jesus Christ. Their sentence will be eternal bondage in hell.

For those who have accepted the forgiveness of Christ, the divine courtroom experience will be much different, indeed. As you rise to stand before the Judge, Jesus will step in front of you and declare, "I took the punishment for her. I paid the price for this one. She is innocent of any wrongdoing. Her reward is to live with Me in heaven forever."

Can you even imagine the untold glory of that moment? We, who were guilty of sin and bound for eternal bondage in hell, are now declared innocent and free by the One who paid the price!

⧗   *How does the above picture strengthen your faith?*

⧗   *Is there some way you would like to respond to the Lord knowing He will declare you as innocent?*

Ages and Stages

As Peter continued to prepare the early church for unthinkable persecution, he was intent on reminding them to stay focused upon the vital issues that truly matter. He reminds all of us who live on the time side of eternity that there is much at stake as we live our lives solely for Christ and not for the culture.

> **The end of all things is near; therefore, be of sound judgment and sober spirit for the purpose of prayer. (1 Peter 4:7)**

As I read the above verse, I realize the principles presented are not just for a suffering church, but they are for men and women in all ages and stages of life. And, as I prayerfully read through those principles again, I realize I am unable to do this in my own strength. I need help to be of sound judgment, to maintain a sober spirit, and to stay grounded in prayer.

Peter, the one who used to speak and then think, now knows the value of thinking before speaking and praying before acting. He learned this difficult lesson during the days when he reprimanded Jesus, cut off a soldier's ear, and even denied the Lord. Peter is intent on preventing others from making the same errors in judgment he had made. As I listen to the plea of Peter, I can hear the tone of his voice begging me—as a modern woman—not to be impetuous in my decision-making and to maintain a wise habit of self-control.

⧖ *Do you struggle with self-control? In what area of your life?*

⧖ *Do you think before you speak? If so, what can you do to change this?*

The Purpose of Prayer

Peter, of all the disciples, realized how dominant the flesh could be in the testing moments of life. I believe Peter vividly remembered what happened in the Garden of Gethsemane when he fell asleep three times while Jesus was praying and sweating great drops of blood. At that moment, when the flesh won in Peter's life, these were the words of Jesus:

> **Keep watching and praying that you may not enter into temptation; the spirit is willing, but the flesh is weak. (Matthew 26:41)**

Peter was well acquainted with the very real pain of giving in to temptation and then later regretting it. Peter had declared his loyalty to Jesus, but instead of praying, he drooled, snored, and slept on. When the time came for Peter to proclaim Jesus, he denied Him three times.

I have always wondered if Peter had prayed rather than slept, would he have had the courage to proclaim Jesus rather than to deny Him? The powerful lesson in this poignant story is that time spent in prayer is a shield against sin. Women who cultivate a vibrant prayer life are not as prone to sin. They also develop the resolve to proclaim the power of the Cross.

Prayer should always be a Christian's greatest delight and most enthusiastic discipline. Prayer is the moment when a believer comes into the presence of our good Father and begins a heartfelt and loving conversation with Him. We talk and He listens—then we listen while He responds to our conversation. To pray is not to merely talk *at* God but it is the beautiful invitation to commune with the Father. Prayer is not a monologue but a dialogue. It is not a soliloquy but a sweet two-sided conversation.

Prayer is filled with exclamations of thanksgiving and gratitude. As you come into the greatest Throne Room in all of eternity, you can boldly request from the Father. You can tell Him what you need and what you desire. Every prayer should close with the submissive words, *Nevertheless, not my will but Your will be done, Father.*

Prayer is a classroom of the highest learning known to humanity. In the classroom of prayer, I have learned that while I am allowed to boldly request, I must also learn to humbly trust.

⧗ *How much time do you set aside daily for prayer?*

⧗ *Do you have a prayer journal?*

⧗ *What have you learned in the classroom of prayer?*

THE MIRROR

Why don't you take a minute and pray for the suffering church? Pray for the men and women around the world who are serving Jesus yet could be killed or imprisoned at any moment. Perhaps there is a particular country you could adopt as your very own and pray daily for this beloved group of believers.

ETERNAL WORDS

Above all, keep fervent in your love for one another, because love covers a multitude of sins. Be hospitable to one another without complaint. As each one has received a special gift, employ it in serving one another as good stewards of the manifold grace of God. (1 Peter 4:8–10)

MY PRAYER FOR TODAY

Jesus, thank You for my life. Thank You for Your protection and for Your love. Lord, today I ask that You teach me how to pray in a dynamic and even historical manner. I pray You would give me a burning desire to spend time with You in the classroom of prayer. In Jesus' name I pray. Amen.

Day 3

The Greatest of These . . .

At the end of our lives, we will no longer care about who weighed the least, who made the most, or who achieved human greatness. When each of our lives pass from time into eternity, our former street address will be unimportant, our marital status will matter no more, and the upward climb on the corporate ladder will seem worthless. What will matter at the end of life is how well we loved those whom we were given. It always comes back to love, doesn't it?

⏳ *Who has loved you the most in your life?*

⏳ *Who have you loved the most?*

Above All

The way we treat one another is paramount in the timeless kingdom of Jesus Christ. He cares deeply about the words we speak, the heart attitudes we embrace, and the actions we exhibit to others.

> **Above all, keep fervent in your love for one another, because love covers a multitude of sins. (1 Peter 4:8)**

According to Peter, the most important choice we make is how we treat others made in the image of the Father. If someone neglects to sweep the kitchen floor—keep your love for each other at full strength. If there is a mess in the family car—fan the flame of love instead of lashing out in frustration. If your birthday is forgotten—celebrate someone else who is lonely. Every other detail in life pales in comparison to the love we give our family, friends, and even strangers.

Peter does not justify, nor does he call us to exhibit just a little bit of love. Rather he begs the Body of Christ to love one another deeply and fully. Of all the habits in life to which you devote time and energy, the most important one is the love you share.

> *"AND YOU SHALL LOVE THE LORD YOUR GOD WITH ALL YOUR HEART, AND WITH ALL YOUR SOUL, AND WITH ALL YOUR MIND, AND WITH ALL YOUR STRENGTH." The second is this, "YOU SHALL LOVE YOUR NEIGHBOR AS YOURSELF." There is no other commandment greater than these.* (Mark 12:30–31)

The most compelling priority in each one of our humble yet meaningful lives is to love without restraint and care about one another enthusiastically. There is no greater command, goal, or purpose than the one to love.

⧗   *Who has been the most difficult person for you to love?*

⧗   *Is it realistic, or sincere, to exhibit love for a person even when you don't feel like it?*

Unconditional Response

> *But now faith, hope, love, abide these three; but the greatest of these is love.* (1 Corinthians 13:13)

The unique call of Christianity is to not only love the lovable, but we are commanded to love even our enemies. We exhibit love when we are mistreated, rejected, and ignored. We maintain fervent love when politics divide, when generations disagree, and when wronged by those in authority. We love on and on and on. It is not only our most important calling, but it is who we are. Love is how we are defined.

> *But love your enemies, and do good, and lend, expecting nothing in return; and your reward will be great, and you will be sons of the Most High; for He Himself is kind to ungrateful and evil men.* (Luke 6:35)

While others are consumed by differences and preferences, we resolve to be God's vessels of unconditional love to a dark and dying world. The most significant and Christlike choice an ordinary man or common woman can make is to love someone whose wounds ooze bitterness and spite. We love not because of personal greatness but we love to become more like Jesus.

> *The one who does not love does not know God, for God is love.* (1 John 4:8)

⧗   *Write your definition of the word love. Make it practical.*

Loving and Lovable

If your heart's desire is to honor God and communicate that you are a woman of deep Christian faith, then you must be both loving and lovable. Your love for people of all races, political persuasions, and socio-economic levels should rise above every other goal and priority in your life. We cannot afford to allow our love for others to slip based on their behavior or to slide when we are disgruntled. Love is verbal and it is action.

We love, because He first loved us. If someone says, "I love God," and hates his brother, he is a liar; for the one who does not love his brother whom he has seen, cannot love God whom he has not seen. And this commandment we have from Him, that the one who loves God should love his brother also. (1 John 4:19–21)

According to Peter who was inspired by the Holy Spirit, our love for one another must flow without ceasing. Our faucet of love should never be turned off or turned down. God's will for your life and mine is our commitment to enthusiastic love when it is easy and when it is difficult.

Love heals brokenness and it covers disappointment. Love instills new hope, and it obliterates bitterness. Love resolves differences and forgives betrayal.

There is nothing love cannot face; there is no limit to its faith, its hope, and its endurance. (1 Corinthians 13:7 NEB)

One of the stirring reasons love is a priority is due to its massive power—love has the ability to cover a multitude of sins. This does not mean love ignores sin. But love does call the offended to treat the offender with compassion and mercy.

Love speaks the truth with great kindness rather than with anger or impatience. When someone is behaving abysmally, love is still able to believe the best. Love always builds up and never tears down.

When Craig and I were raising our family of five creative, opinionated, strong-willed children, I reminded them often, "In this family we build—we never destroy. We build with our words and our actions. How could you build up your sister? How could you encourage your brother?"

⌛ *What does it mean to "build up" rather than "tear down" in the home or in family relationships?*

⏳ *Specifically dealing with speech patterns, what should be allowed in family relationships and what should not be allowed?*

True Love

Often, when I find I am unable to love someone with my own strength, I must remember that true agape love flows from my relationship with Jesus Christ. If I am struggling to love a man or woman whom God loves deeply, I make the choice to spend more time in prayer and in Bible reading. I go to Jesus to find the source of love not in my human nature. If I truly desire to become more like Him, I must have more of Him. I must spend time in Christ's presence and turn up the heat of my love for Him. As I love Jesus with greater intentionality, my love for others begins to boil again.

I am often unable to love from my flesh, but I can always love from His Spirit. When my love for others is ebbing away, if I focus on fresh passion for Christ, I soon discover that while I am unable He is more than able. When I am weak in love, He can become strong in me.

⏳ *Do you believe that stirring up your love for Christ can enable you to love challenging people? Why or why not?*

THE MIRROR

⏳ *What makes a person easy to love? List three characteristics that make a person lovable:*

1. _____

2. _____

3. _____

Now hold yourself up to that measuring stick. Do others consider you lovable or not?

ETERNAL WORDS

Above all, keep fervent in your love for one another, because love covers a multitude of sins. Be hospitable to one another without complaint. As each one has received a special gift, employ it in serving one another as good stewards of the manifold grace of God. (1 Peter 4:8–10)

MY PRAYER FOR TODAY

Jesus, I come to You humbly yet desperately today. I have fallen so short in my capacity to love other people. I am intensely aware of how much I need You to help me love others the way You have loved me. Help me to love, Jesus. Help me. In Your name I pray. Amen.

Day 4

No Complaining Allowed!

As you already know, I attended a Christian university and was deeply impacted by the campus chaplain, Brother Bob Stamps. He was a bachelor for most of my years at the university until God brought an amazing woman into his life when he was in his mid-thirties.

Corrie ten Boom spoke at the chapel service during the fall semester of my junior year and stayed for a series of meetings. Corrie's traveling companion was a beautiful Dutch nurse who instantly captured Brother Bob's heart. They married the following summer.

All the students watched Bob and Ellen's life with interest and a little bit of jealousy–their union seemed ordained by heaven. We all yearned for an invitation to their uniquely European home, hoping to bask in the wonder of their love. We also wanted to drink in Ellen's rich blend of hospitality and charm.

Upon arrival, classical music gently played in the background as their front door opened to an atmosphere that assailed every sense. Ellen displayed fresh flowers artistically throughout the rooms of her home, scented candles burned, and framed scripture verses decorated this unmatched place of love, joy, and laughter.

One evening, shortly after I married Craig, I arrived early to help Ellen prepare for the fifty or so students arriving after the Friday evening communion service. We went to the grocery store to purchase supplies. I was surprised when she picked flowers out of the nearly dead bouquets.

"Yah, Carol," she said in her lilting Dutch accent. "Never pay full price for flowers. Always buy the ones about to be thrown away for half price."

At the house, Ellen asked me to check on the pies browning in the oven. As I opened the oven door, five perfect apple pies awaited display on the dining room table. "Ellen," I exclaimed, "how in the world did you have time to make these absolutely perfect pies?"

"Oh," she said with a twinkle in her blue eyes, "Mrs. Smith came over to help me."

I never dreamed her delectables came from the frozen food section.

I learned from watching Ellen that hospitality doesn't have to be demanding to look lovely. Nor should the hostess deal with needless stress and self-imposed perfection. Through Ellen's example, I learned entertaining others can bring joy not only to the guests but also to the one who offers the warmth of home, food, and endearing fellowship.

Make Yourself at Home

Peter presents a practical, life-giving assignment in the series of verses we are studying.

> *The end of all things is near; therefore, be of sound judgment and sober spirit for the purpose of prayer. Above all, keep fervent in your love for one another, because love covers a multitude of sins. Be hospitable to one another without complaint.* (1 **Peter 4:7–9**)

As we commit our lives to prayer, it produces a fervent love for those in our lives. This love demonstrates itself with a heart attitude rejoicing in the opportunity to serve one another through the loveliness of hospitality.

The Greek word for hospitality is *philoxenos*, which means "to be fond of guests or to be a lover of hospitality." Hospitality, therefore, is not a "have to" but a "get to" for those who love the Lord and are determined to obey His unchanging Word. Hospitality prioritizes sharing with others what God has graciously given to you. Hospitality includes the giving of your home, your food, your resources, and an unselfish piece of your heart.

⏳ *Do you enjoy having people in your home? Why or why not?*

Excuses

Many women in the twenty-first century mistakenly believe they don't have time for hospitality, but the truth is we all have time for the things we prioritize. If hospitality becomes important because the Word of God commands it, you realize you not only have the time but the desire to serve the Lord and the Body of Christ in this splendid manner.

There are many women who might believe their house isn't nice enough to invite guests in. I can assure you that hospitality was never meant to be a show-and-tell of who has the most gorgeous home or who is the best cook. Hospitality is the invitation to show love in action to the people whose paths have intersected with yours. When you invite someone into your home, the silent words you are speaking are the welcome mat everyone yearns to experience. Hospitality quietly declares you care about someone, that you desire to spend time with them, and share what has been given to you by the Lord.

Craig, my husband, has pastored many churches over the four decades of our marriage. When our children were little, toys were everywhere, our furniture was either hand-me-downs or garage-sale-specials, and our budget was miniscule. And yet, Craig and I still loved to have people in our home on a weekly basis. I learned to fix simple and inexpensive meals such as spaghetti, day-old bread that became yummy garlic bread, and a tossed salad. Often, dessert was nothing more than whatever cookies were on sale at the store that week. People didn't come for my gourmet cooking—they wanted to be with us. They wanted to laugh with us, play family games, and pray together.

There were times when I was unable to afford even a simple meal for guests, so rather than extending an invitation for a meal, we invited them for snacks and a game night. Popcorn drizzled with chocolate chips became one of my well-known specialties.

You might feel you are not a good cook, but, my friend, you don't need to be Martha Stewart, Betty Crocker, or Rachael Ray to let the love of Jesus shine in your home. Open the door and invite other families to bring a dish to pass. Or, have everyone pitch in financially and order pizza and wings. There were times when Craig and I had people in our home several times a week and I fixed the same menu every time. (This worked out well for me until one of my children told the guests we had eaten the same meal three times that week.) I have learned the word *gourmet* is found nowhere in the definition of *hospitality*.

⧗   *What are some of the excuses you have made in reference to hospitality?*

Entertaining vs. Hospitality

There is a marked difference between the concept of entertaining and the heart of hospitality.

Entertaining focuses on the hostess, the home, and the food. If you entertain guests, your home must be spotless and gorgeous, the food must be exquisite and sumptuous, and you, the hostess, must not only look beautiful but appear in total control.

Hospitality, on the other hand, has its focus on the guests, their comfort, and their needs. A woman who feels the call to hospitality offers people a comfortable place to stay, food that nourishes their bodies as well as their souls, a listening ear, and a loving heart.

> ⧖ *Now that you know the difference, have you primarily entertained people in your home or have you responded to the call of hospitality?*

Inviting Jesus

As you humbly but seriously consider the call to hospitality, perhaps these well-known scriptures will remind you of hospitality's timeless reach:

> *"For I was hungry, and you gave Me something to eat; I was thirsty, and you gave Me something to drink; I was a stranger, and you invited Me in; naked, and you clothed Me; I was sick, and you visited Me; I was in prison, and you came to Me." Then the righteous will answer Him, "Lord, when did we see You hungry, and feed You, or thirsty, and give You something to drink? And when did we see You a stranger, and invite You in, or naked, and clothe You? When did we see You sick, or in prison, and come to You?" The King will answer and say to them, "Truly I say to you, to the extent that you did it to one of these brothers of Mine, even the least of them, you did it to Me." (Matthew 25:35–40)*

When a woman responds to the call of hospitality, she is inviting Jesus into her home. As we open our homes and our hearts to a world in pain, we are extending the invitation of love to Christ Jesus. I dare not turn Him away.

⏳ *Who is the most hospitable person you know? Why?*

Be Very Careful

One of the biggest challenges for me in responding to the call of hospitality is not how I treat the guests but how I treat my family as we prepare for the guests. I must be committed to loving, joyful behavior as I prepare to offer our home. If I have an ill-spirit or am impatient with my children or my husband, I am not obeying Scripture. I must demonstrate hospitality without complaint. I must have a happy heart from the day the invitation is sent until the moment when the cleanup is complete. I must not grumble or complain, express frustration to my husband, or show a short temper to my children.

If we are hospitable only because we "have" to be, it will quickly become legalism and hypocrisy. Authentic Christianity must pervade the ordinary days of life and we must resolve to provide a breath of fresh air to the world.

You may not be called to the mission field, but you are called to show hospitality to your neighbors. You may not feel called to teach a Bible study, but you are called by the Holy Spirit to use your home as a showcase for the love of Christ.

THE MIRROR

⏳ *Do you naturally exhibit the gift of hospitality or is it a challenge for you? Why do you believe Peter places such an emphasis on this one component of calling?*

ETERNAL WORDS

Above all, keep fervent in your love for one another, because love covers a multitude of sins. Be hospitable to one another without complaint. As each one has received a special gift, employ it in serving one another as good stewards of the manifold grace of God. (1 Peter 4:8–10)

MY PRAYER FOR TODAY

Dear Jesus, would You give me the strength and desire to use my home as a spiritual hospital for those in need? Would You open not only the door of my home but also the door of my heart to welcome in a world in pain? Thank You, Lord, that Your ways are always the best. In Your name I pray. Amen.

Day 5

Unwrapping Your Gift

What is the most valuable gift you have ever received? As you already know, someone gave a brand-new car to my daughter upon her return from the mission field. What an incredible present.

Has anyone ever given you a home? It almost seems preposterous, doesn't it? When my husband and I were in the middle of our busiest years, raising children, pastoring a church, homeschooling, and trying to make ends meet, we had outgrown our snug, 1,500-square-foot home. Not only was the home too small for our family of seven, but it was also falling apart. The rear wall of the home was rotting and about to cave in. We needed a new home quickly but lacked the finances.

At the same time we were in need of a home, one of Craig's high school friends was about to list his 3,300-square-foot home. It was a Williamsburg home in a breathtaking setting. This three-story brick residence sat on four acres of picturesque woods and gardens, with a creek running through it. He wanted us to look, knowing we were unable to afford it. It was more than $100,000 dollars out of our price range.

I had a bad attitude (imagine that!) and didn't want to take the time or spend the emotional energy looking at this dream home. We had struggled with finances over the years and I was determined not to want things I was unable to afford.

Craig and my mom were convinced we should at least see this lovely home, so I submitted to their pleading. After we walked through, I was in love. I fell head over heels in love with this gorgeous piece of real estate tens of thousands of dollars above my price range.

The next day, the owner called Craig and came down nearly $100,000 from the asking price. Craig said, "We love your home. We would love to live in it, but we still can't afford it."

Then this man of God did some refiguring and called Craig back later in the day. He then offered to sell it to us for $40,000 less than the last offer. Craig respectfully responded that although his generosity was unmatched, it was still impossible for us to make it work.

The following day, this wonderful, generous man called Craig one more time and said, "If I give you $20,000 for the down payment, could you afford it then?"

We knew we could afford the home with this final offer, but we still had to sell our home, which was in no condition to put on the market.

We were stunned when the unselfish friend of Craig's added, "Go ahead and move in to my home, but we won't close until you sell your old house. I will loan you $50,000 to make the repairs on your current place. When you sell your home, we can close on the new one. Until we close on our transaction, you don't need to pay rent, just utilities."

We were stunned. Who does that?! Who gives a gift so rare and benevolent that it seems unbelievable? God does that. He gives gifts of the rarest and most life-changing kind.

⌛   *What is the most incredible and undeserved tangible gift you have received?*

⌛   *What is the most magnificent tangible gift you have ever given to someone?*

A Delicious Surprise

You have a God-given gift. Everyone does! When God was doling out divine talents for human use, you were not forgotten nor were you overlooked. You were created for a very specific reason of God's own design. When He created you, His plans for your one-of-a-kind life did not include gathering dust or sitting on some obscure shelf. You were created to engage enthusiastically in a grand story written by His hand. You were not designed to be a mere participant, clapping for others who seem to have the starring roles. You were not formed to watch while others made a profound difference in the epic history of God's people. You, my friend, are the difference-maker, the image-bearer, and the gift itself.

> *As each one has received a special gift, employ it in serving one another as good stewards of the manifold grace of God.* **(1 Peter 4:10)**

Peter is extremely clear that everyone is a recipient of the delightful endowment God bestowed upon His children. I believe a rich part of the abundant life we are given on earth is to discover the talents, abilities, and purpose assigned to us. Unwrapping the captivating and strategic gift that is ours is like going on an adventure hunt and uncovering a treasure chest of gold. The thrill is not only in what we receive, but also in the journey of discovery. As you search for God and His righteousness, unearth a delicious surprise meant only for you.

⌛ *Before you read any further, what personal gift do you believe God has given you?*

⌛ *Is there a gift you wish He would give you? (I have always wanted to sing like Sandi Patty or Karen Carpenter, but wasn't given that specific talent.)*

Purposeful Gifts

When God bestows a gift, it comes with a specific purpose. We are to use our God-given talents to help one another and make someone's life easier, because we are in it.

> *Since we have gifts that differ according to the grace given to us, each of us is to exercise them accordingly: if prophecy, according to the proportion of his faith; if service, in his serving; or he who teaches, in his teaching; or he who exhorts, in his exhortation; he who gives, with liberality; he who leads, with diligence; he who shows mercy, with cheerfulness.* (**Romans 12:6–8**)

The abilities that are now ours, because of the benevolence of the Father, are not for our self-enjoyment or for the building up of our own egos. God's plan encompasses pieces of His character, wrapped by the Holy Spirit, for the express goal of encouraging someone else. The gift is actually not *for* us but it does come *through* us to benefit a world in pain.

The following scripture passage is lengthy, but I want you to prayerfully read through it and circle the specific talent you believe is yours through the power of God. (If you would like to learn more about spiritual gifts, you could also read the entire chapter of Romans 12.)

> *Now concerning spiritual gifts, brethren, I do not want you to be unaware.*
>
> *Now there are varieties of gifts, but the same Spirit. And there are varieties of ministries, and the same Lord. There are varieties of effects, but the same God who works all things in all persons. But to each one is given the manifestation of the Spirit for the common good. For to one is given the word of wisdom through the Spirit, and to another the word of knowledge according to the same Spirit; to another faith by the same Spirit, and to another gifts of healing by the one Spirit, and to another the effecting of miracles, and to another prophecy, and to another the distinguishing of spirits, to another various kinds of tongues, and to another the interpretation of tongues. But one and the same Spirit works all these things, distributing to each one individually just as He wills* (**1 Corinthians 12:1, 4–11**).

We need to remain aware of a most important personal aspect of sharing one's gift with the Body of Christ. We must never compare our gifting with another's talent, nor should we allow jealousy to grow in our hearts. God has given the gift and we must thank Him for ours, while celebrating those of others. We must use the gift for His glory and to encourage.

And He gave some as apostles, and some as prophets, and some as evangelists, and some as pastors and teachers, for the equipping of the saints for the work of service, to the building up of the body of Christ; until we all attain to the unity of the faith, and of the knowledge of the Son of God, to a mature man, to the measure of the stature which belongs to the fullness of Christ. (Ephesians 4:11–13)

Speaking and Serving

Many of the gifts God has entrusted us with are connected to speaking or serving. Honestly, we all speak, and we all serve daily, so we must pay careful attention to the forthcoming advice of Peter:

Whoever speaks, is to do so as one who is speaking the utterances of God; whoever serves is to do so as one who is serving by the strength which God supplies; so that in all things God may be glorified through Jesus Christ, to whom belongs the glory and dominion forever and ever. Amen. (1 Peter 4:11)

In Peter's reference to speaking, he does not just mean public speaking, but refers to any conversation in which we might engage. Peter's high standard concerning speech makes my heart beat rapidly and causes me to close my eyes in personal embarrassment. At times, I have not verbalized *one speaking the utterances of God*. More often, I have spoken with the utterances of Carol, also known as my opinion.

From this day forward, I must resolve to only communicate what my good Father in heaven would say. As I consider God's speech patterns, I know He doesn't talk excessively, and He never panics. He is always wise and loving with His statements and He is never overly emotional. God always tells the truth and His chief intent is to encourage rather than discourage. God looks for the best, believes for the best, and speaks the best over His beloved children. I can do no less.

The call to service provides a wonderful opportunity to tap into the power of God rather than merely relying on your own strength. If you insist on serving others with your own strength or for your own self-esteem, you will soon grow weary and resentful. But as we are called into a partnership with the One who gave us our gift, it is His unselfish and supernatural strength that will empower our service for His honor and glory.

THE MIRROR

⧗ *What is your most valuable possession? Think about it for a minute and then write it below.*

⧗ *Would you ever be willing to sell this possession? Why or why not? For what price?*

ETERNAL WORDS

Above all, keep fervent in your love for one another, because love covers a multitude of sins. Be hospitable to one another without complaint. As each one has received a special gift, employ it in serving one another as good stewards of the manifold grace of God. (1 Peter 4:8–10)

MY PRAYER FOR TODAY

Holy Spirit, thank You for the amazing gift You have given me. I pray that as I use it to encourage others, You will use me to make hell smaller and heaven bigger. I pray my life will leave an imprint of the compassion and love of Jesus Christ. In Jesus' name I pray. Amen.

Week 9

Keep On Rejoicing!

Day 1

No Surprise!

Apprehended by the Holy Spirit, Peter was intent on returning to the subject of suffering in his heartfelt letter to the early church. Followers of "The Way" were beheaded, burned at the stake, fed to lions, and scattered across the ancient world. Peter knew God was not surprised by any human happening. God has an eternal plan that trumps suffering, is victorious against evil empires, and comforts those who are oppressed. If God is not surprised, why should we be?

⏳ *When you see the storm clouds of suffering gathering on the horizon of your life, what is your immediate emotional response? Be honest.*

Focus on Faith

As Christians, we will encounter trials during our time on earth. Peter heard Jesus speak these very words just before they went to the Garden of Gethsemane with James and John:

> **These things I have spoken to you, so that in Me you may have peace. In the world you have tribulation, but take courage; I have overcome the world. (John 16:33)**

The words of Jesus and the heart of Peter should prepare every Christian for suffering. It *will* be part of our story—so don't be surprised.

> **Beloved, do not be surprised at the fiery ordeal among you, which comes upon you for your testing, as though some strange thing were happening to you. (1 Peter 4:12)**

As believers in Jesus Christ, we are assured of a certainty—we will experience trials in life. However, we are also assured of His presence, His love, His protection, and His appointment. Our initial response to distress and affliction should never include bewilderment as though something extraordinary were happening. As I ponder the men and women in Scripture whom God used in a significant manner, they all carried the experience of tribulation with them.

- **Shadrach, Meshach, and Abednego** spent time in the fiery furnace.
- **Esther's** entire race was threatened with annihilation.
- **Moses** faced the Egyptians, the Red Sea, and the wilderness.
- **Noah** knew the entire population of the planet, other than his family, would be killed by a great flood.
- **Ruth's** husband died, she moved to a foreign country with her mother-in-law, and lived in poverty.
- **Daniel** spent the night in a lions' den with large, ravenous felines.
- **Jonah** spent three days in the belly of a great fish.
- **Sarah and Hannah** dealt with decades of infertility.
- **David** faced a giant.
- **Paul and Silas** spent time in a Roman jail.

All these men and women of faith left a legacy of joy and hope despite the suffering they endured. We learn from their example and develop the determination to keep our eyes firmly fixed on Jesus who has gone before us.

> *God will not permit any troubles to come upon us, unless He has a specific plan by which great blessing can come out of the difficulty.*
>
> —Peter Marshall

⌛ *Have you seen anything good come out of your days of suffering? What good was produced?*

Rejoice!

Peter offers a healthier response to suffering.

> *But to the degree that you share the sufferings of Christ, keep on rejoicing, so that also at the revelation of His glory you may rejoice with exultation.* (1 Peter 4:13)

What a vibrant, powerful response to the surety that sufferings will be part of our human experience! When others complain and grumble—we are the ones who rejoice. When people panic and give in to despair—we sing louder. When folks wail and scream—we lift our hands in the air and keep our eyes on Jesus.

I must tell you this series of verses is among my favorites in the entire New Testament. This is our game plan for trials—we keep on rejoicing. We choose joy when joy, in the natural, would be our last human response. We open our mouths and worship the Father even though there may be tears running down our cheeks. A trial or suffering is never a reason to stop singing. Trauma or pain should instigate a louder song, deeper worship, and resolute praise.

We rejoice not because of the trial but in response to God's power, His provision, His love, and His promises. We are among the very strange group of people who . . . *consider it all joy when you encounter various trials* (James 1:2).

There are times we will scratch our heads and look toward heaven with questions in our hearts, but deep within our souls, have the assurance that suffering is a cause for joy. Our tenacious grasp on worship will deliver the stubborn and strengthening joy that was always meant to be ours in the middle of a trial.

⧖ *List three practical ways you can exhibit the joy of the Lord when going through a trial:*

1. _____

2. _____

3. _____

Reasons

> *If you are reviled for the name of Christ, you are blessed, because the Spirit of glory and of God rests on you. Make sure that none of you*

suffers as a murderer, or thief, or evildoer, or a troublesome meddler;
but if anyone suffers as a Christian, he is not to be ashamed, but is to
glorify God in this name. **(1 Peter 4:14–16)**

If the suffering you encounter is instigated because of your faith in Christ, you are guaranteed an extraordinary blessing. The Spirit of God will be visible in your life as you choose to honor the Lord rather than the culture, your family, or even yourself.

Suffering is not a reason to feel ashamed or embarrassed, but provides an opportunity to allow the glory of God to leak out of your own glorious life. As you suffer, lift your hands toward heaven and ask for more of His character to be demonstrated through you.

When Peter penned the sobering yet brilliant words in 1 Peter, he did not know that he, like his Savior, would be crucified upon a cross. However, Peter chose to be crucified upside down, because he did not feel worthy to die in the same manner as the One he so loved—Jesus Christ.

THE MIRROR

⧗ *I believe suffering gives us the opportunity to share a rich, eternal experience with Jesus. Suffering refines us in a way nothing else can. How has suffering refined you over the years?*

ETERNAL WORDS

Beloved, do not be surprised at the fiery ordeal among you, which comes upon you for your testing, as though some strange thing were happening to you; but to the degree that you share the sufferings of Christ, keep on rejoicing, so that also at the revelation of His glory you may rejoice with exultation. **(1 Peter 4:12–13)**

MY PRAYER FOR TODAY

Dear Jesus, I love You so much and I count it an honor to suffer for You and with You. Give me strength, Father, for the days ahead, and help me to use my pain to increase your kingdom. In Jesus' name I pray. Amen.

Day 2

Turn It Around

Let's face it—none of us enjoys suffering. We aren't thrilled when a trial invades our human existence. However, there is a godly, holy, and healthy way to turn the flames of affliction into our finest hour. Suffering, when committed to Christ, offers an opportunity to show a powerful witness for God's unchanging faithfulness and perpetual goodness. As we suffer, and we surely will, the world is watching. We must show people how to lay hold of joy amidst sorrow and exemplify how to worship in the storm.

An Awful Word

For it is time for judgment to begin with the household of God; and if it begins with us first, what will be the outcome for those who do not obey the gospel of God? AND IF IT IS WITH DIFFICULTY THAT THE RIGHTEOUS IS SAVED, WHAT WILL BECOME OF THE GODLESS MAN AND THE SINNER? (1 Peter 4:17–18)

The word judgment is a perfectly awful word, isn't it? I don't like to feel judged and I try valiantly not to judge others. However, the Word explains that God has that authority. He carries the right to judge not only those who have come to Christ, but also those who have refused His love and forgiveness.

For a believer, judgment can take on many forms and various purposes, but the end goal is always a refining process. I am judged by my perfect Father so I will refrain from sin and live a righteous life that honors only Him and not self. True maturity is apparent in a Christian's life when we willingly choose to judge ourselves before God must intervene.

When I know I am spending too much money and then choose to cut up my credit cards, I am judging myself, and therein I find freedom and victory. If God intervenes in judgment, and my spending causes friction in my marriage or with creditors, it becomes much more painful.

There is no fear of judgment for the man who judges himself according to the Word of God.

—Howard G. Hendricks

Peter asks two horrible questions in these two verses, both of which likely have the same answer.

"What will be the outcome for those who do not obey the Gospel?"
"What will become of the godless man and the sinner?"

Even as I read those two devastating questions, my heart is filled with the names of those whom I love dearly but have not yet come to a saving knowledge of Jesus Christ. What will become of them? My heart aches with both compassion and dread knowing the answer.

These two verses, and thus these two questions, do not scare me, but they compel me to tell the story of Jesus. These two questions remind me I must live my life to honor the Lord as a living sacrifice for the timeless kingdom of Christ. I must make use of every opportunity to speak of my faith and to present the principles of salvation to a world who faces a terrible eternity without Christ.

⧗   *How do the two verses about judgment impact your heart?*

⧗   *Is there anything for which you should judge yourself? How so?*

Faithful

I love the Word of God, and I deeply desire that you fall in love as well. Oh! How I long for you to open the sacred pages of Scripture. You will experience His power streaming into your heart. I pray as you settle in and read timeless truth, you will feel stunned and grateful by God's personal message. I pray when a verse touches you deeply, your heart will beat rapidly and you will inhale His goodness and wisdom.

There are verses in the Bible that simply take my breath away and cause my jaw to hang slack at the wisdom therein. The following verse is one of them. As I meditate upon this passage, I think of all the heroes and heroines of faith who have gone before me and have served the Lord with willing sacrifice and uncommon selflessness. I long to be counted among their number–those found faithful in suffering.

> *Therefore, those also who suffer according to the will of God shall entrust their souls to a faithful Creator in doing what is right.* (1 Peter 4:19)

This verse does not imply that suffering *is* the will of God for His children, but it does state that when you encounter suffering, you should always live according to the will and purposes of God. God has a blueprint for us to follow when pain enters our world. Perhaps the following list will remind you of God's plan. I'll title it, *How to Suffer Well.*

- Rejoice loudly
- Refuse to complain or panic
- Count it all joy
- Walk by faith and not by sight
- Ask the Holy Spirit to give you His divine power
- Refuse to be afraid
- Take every thought captive to the obedience of Christ
- Live righteously—don't give in to moral compromise
- Continue to tithe and serve others
- Stay in the Word of God
- Pray continually
- Keep your eyes and heart set on Jesus not on the suffering

God has a profound and priceless blessing hidden among the folds of affliction.

You can trust your faithful Creator. He is still on the throne even when your world is troubled. You can trust your good, good Father—He is not surprised by the distress that surrounds you. You can be assured He is still in control and He has never lost a battle yet.

Most Important Word

The most important word in 1 Peter 4:19 is stunning . . . it is the word *entrust*. We are among the thousands upon thousands of men and women who have entrusted our souls—our very lives—to a faithful God.

The trust we have placed in God helps us overcome the needless emotion of fear. As we trust Him, fear will flee, and His sweet peace that passes all human understanding will remain.

> *The steadfast of mind You will keep in perfect peace, Because he trusts in You.* (Isaiah 26:3)

> *When I am afraid, I will put my trust in You.* (Psalm 56:3)

The choice to trust God, especially during times of suffering, will enable you to conquer foreboding emotions and capture unfounded feelings. If you need more joy, the answer lies in your determinate to trust the Lord.

> *But let all those rejoice who put their trust in You;*
> *Let them ever shout for joy, because You defend them;*
> *Let those also who love Your name*
> *Be joyful in You.* (Psalm 5:11 NKJV)

⧖ *What does it mean to you that your God is faithful?*

⧗ As you read the items on the list of "How to Suffer Well," is there anything you would add to this list?

THE MIRROR

⧗ Why do you believe suffering is a part of the human experience? Is there a reason God does not always remove pain from our lives?

ETERNAL WORDS

Beloved, do not be surprised at the fiery ordeal among you, which comes upon you for your testing, as though some strange thing were happening to you; but to the degree that you share the sufferings of Christ, keep on rejoicing, so that also at the revelation of His glory you may rejoice with exultation. (1 Peter 4:12–13)

MY PRAYER FOR TODAY

Lord Jesus, I don't want to suffer, but if I do, I pray I will honor You every day, every hour, and every minute. I can joyfully entrust my soul to You knowing You are faithful and You love me. In Jesus' name I pray. Amen.

Day 3

Leaders Lead

Are you willing to stand up for your faith? Are you willing to say, "Yes! I am a Christian," to people who mock your faith, scorn your convictions, and ridicule your behavior? The world has been infiltrated by the enemy of the cross of Christ and this enemy's voice is rampant in education, entertainment, and politics. We are not the only generation, nor will we be the last, called upon to make a public and unrelenting stand for Jesus. We must make our faith known by the words we speak, the way we treat others, the choices we make, and the convictions we hold.

⌛ *When was the last time you told a nonbeliever about Jesus Christ?*

⌛ *Have you ever led someone to Christ?*

Everyone a Leader

In this final chapter, Peter begins by addressing the leaders in the early church. As we process his words and message, it is vital to remember we are all a leader to someone. Mothers lead their children while teachers lead their classrooms. The older women are called to lead younger women by example and words. The more mature in the Lord should be discipling and encouraging those who are new in the faith. Employers lead employees and grandmothers lead grandchildren. As Christians, we are called to be servant-leaders to the world in which we live.

> *Therefore, I exhort the elders among you, as your fellow elder and witness of the sufferings of Christ, and a partaker also of the glory that is to be revealed.* (**1 Peter 5:1**)

We now know, with our brothers and sisters in Christ from the early church, that our sufferings join us to the heart of Christ. We are also poignantly aware of the fellowship it produces—both genuine and sobering. Not only do we share the sufferings of Christ, but we are also given the gift of His glory to share with others. We are not to magnify self but light the way as a beacon, leading others to Him.

⏳ *Who are you currently leading with your words and by your example?*

⏳ *What does it mean that we are "a partaker of the glory that is to be revealed"?*

Tend My Sheep

Our must profound calling as leaders is to take care of people tenderly and compassionately. We are not army drill sergeants who boss, yell, and punish. We are not slave-owners who demand, compel, and mistreat. We are shepherds who are thoughtfully concerned about those under our watch.

> *Shepherd the flock of God among you, exercising oversight not under compulsion, but voluntarily, according to the will of God; and not for*

sordid gain, but with eagerness; nor yet as lording it over those allotted to your charge, but proving to be examples to the flock. **(1 Peter 5:2–3)**

Peter chose the phrase *"shepherd the flock of God among you"* as he spoke to the leaders in the early church concerning their expected behavior. The word *shepherd* is the Greek word *poimaino*, which means "to shepherd, to tend, to take care of, to pastor." This was also the very word Jesus spoke to Peter when He met with the disciples after His resurrection.

> *So when they had finished breakfast, Jesus said to Simon Peter, "Simon, son of John, do you love Me more than these?" He said to Him, "Yes, Lord; You know that I love You." He said to him, "Tend My lambs." He said to him again a second time, "Simon, son of John, do you love Me?" He said to Him, "Yes, Lord; You know that I love You." He said to him, "Shepherd My sheep." He said to him the third time, "Simon, son of John, do you love Me?" Peter was grieved because He said to him the third time, "Do you love Me?" And he said to Him, "Lord, You know all things; You know that I love You." Jesus said to him, "Tend My sheep." (John 21:15–17)*

Jesus appointed Peter as a shepherd of the flock over every believer and now we receive that same assignment as well. The word *poimaino* also means "oversight that produces nourishment." Every believer in Christ is called to lead people to nourishing places from which to feed, allowing growth to happen.

As servant-leaders in the Body of Christ, we must fulfill this duty enthusiastically and cheerfully. When the children's director needs volunteers in the nursery or in Sunday school, apply 1 Peter 5:2–3 to your life. When the church seeks people willing to open their homes for small groups or for missionaries, apply 1 Peter 5:2–3 to the call. When the church needs cleaning, meals need prepared, greeters need to greet, or the youth group needs chaperones, apply 1 Peter 5:2–3.

There is only one way to truly lead and serve—with pure joy and fervent love.

⧗   *Who is the Lord calling you to lead?*

⧗   *Who is the Lord calling you to serve?*

⧗   *Why do some of us have such a difficult time responding to these very practical needs within the church?*

Benefit Package

Peter warns us not to desire leadership in the Body of Christ as a means of becoming rich or enhancing earthly power. In this next section, however, Peter eagerly tells of the payment we will receive in eternity.

> **And when the Chief Shepherd appears, you will receive the unfading crown of glory. (1 Peter 5:4)**

You might feel as if the Lord doesn't see your service or your suffering, but He does. The reward for faithful service and for uncomplaining affliction will likely not happen in this life. But it is guaranteed in your heavenly home. When God gives a reward, it is never attached to a temporary or tangible citizenship, but it will last for all of eternity. The blessing the Father has for you will go on and on and on. It is timeless!

Today as you serve, don't expect a thank you note, but know there is a blessing beyond imagination awaiting you in heaven. And, if today you are suffering, continue to worship the One who created You and remain more aware of His presence than you are of your pain.

THE MIRROR

⧗ *As you serve the Body of Christ, check your heart attitude. Are you doing it willingly and enthusiastically?*

⧗ *List three adjectives that in your opinion describe heaven:*

1. _____

2. _____

3. _____

ETERNAL WORDS

Beloved, do not be surprised at the fiery ordeal among you, which comes upon you for your testing, as though some strange thing were happening to you; but to the degree that you share the sufferings of Christ, keep on rejoicing, so that also at the revelation of His glory you may rejoice with exultation. (1 Peter 4:12–13)

MY PRAYER FOR TODAY

Jesus, thank You for calling me to servant-leadership in your amazing church. Help me to be humble and kind as I serve. Father, I pray You will give me the gift of encouragement so I am able to lift up those who are suffering today. In Jesus' name I pray. Amen.

Day 4

Wrapped In Humility

One of my earthly treasures is found in a plastic container filled with aprons. They were each made by either my precious Aunt Marianne or by my Grandma Boyce. My mom wasn't much of a seamstress so every Christmas and Mother's Day, she was given an apron made by either her sister or her mother. They are quintessential aprons from the 1950s and 1960s. A few of them have rickrack around the edges. These were my mother's "everyday" aprons. Some of these family heirlooms are trimmed with white lace and are made of organza. As you can imagine, these were my mom's Sunday or holiday kitchen coverings.

Each time I open the container and reverently take one out, I picture my mother dancing around the kitchen with my father or carefully frosting her famous angel food cake with airy whipped cream. I can almost smell Sunday dinner complete with roast beef, mashed potatoes, green beans, and apple pie. My fabric treasures mean little to anyone but me.

These aprons are a symbol of my mother's great love for her family and how she served us willingly and joyfully. They are also symbolic of another time in history, when the home was the center of culture and a woman's identity was tied to her apron.

⧗   *Do you have any earthly treasures or family heirlooms? What are they?*

⧗   *What do these treasures represent to you?*

Humility

If you want to be like Jesus, you will wrap yourself in the character trait of humility. An act of will that does not come from our human nature, humility is the simple yet focused choice to dress like our elder brother, Jesus.

> *You younger men, likewise, be subject to your elders; and all of you, clothe yourselves with humility toward one another, for GOD IS OPPOSED TO THE PROUD, BUT GIVES GRACE TO THE HUMBLE.*
>
> *Therefore humble yourselves under the mighty hand of God, that He may exalt you at the proper time.* (1 Peter 5:5–6)

Peter beseeches the early, suffering church to clothe themselves with humility in their human relationships. Humility is the key to a healthy family, a flourishing marriage, a unified church, and peace in human relationships. Someone must choose to stay humble. That someone is you.

The word for clothing Peter uses is actually the word for apron—only servants wore this piece of clothing. The aprons at that time in history were not decorated with ruffles nor were they meant to make a fashion statement. Aprons worn by first-century servants were made of plain, sturdy fabric and were large enough to wrap around one's entire body. The aprons were so large that not one piece of their own garment showed.

We, as servants in the Body of Christ, are expected to wear a replica of this apron. You and I should be so wrapped in humility that not one iota of self is seen by the world around us. We must choose to put on this serviceable, nondescript garment and it must stay visible in every situation. Humility is more than a good idea, or a trait admired in someone else, it is a choice we each must make daily.

Humility is embracing a humble opinion of oneself or lowliness of mind. Humility is birthed in our minds and then seeps into our speech patterns and our actions. Peter commands his brothers and sisters to *humble yourself*.

If you humble yourself, God will exalt you when the time is right. However, don't confuse your job description with that of the Father's—you do the humbling and allow Him to do the exalting. If you exalt yourself, it's guaranteed that God will then do the humbling. If you elevate yourself, God will likely allow the circumstances of life to humble you.

As a daughter of your loving and compassionate Father, you don't need to waste one minute worrying about your position or status. It's not necessary to strive for the proper recognition you believe you might deserve. God's recognition is so much more precious and valuable than the applause of men. If you continue to serve the Body of Christ, wearing the apron of humility, God will bless you and lift you up at just the right time. It's a promise.

⧖   *Who is the humblest person you know?*

⧖   *How do they exhibit this character trait of humility?*

The Team Uniform

When we choose to clothe ourselves with humility, we are dressing just like our elder brother. We are, in effect, wearing the team uniform that identifies our relationship with Jesus.

> *Have this attitude in yourselves which was also in Christ Jesus, who, although He existed in the form of God, did not regard equality with God a thing to be grasped, but emptied Himself, taking the form of a bond-servant, and being made in the likeness of men. Being found in appearance as a man, He humbled Himself by becoming obedient to the point of death, even death on a cross. (Philippians 2:5–8)*

⧖   *These verses remind us that Jesus exhibited humility by His death on a cross. How else did He exhibit humility?*

He Cares

The following scripture is so lovely, and has so much tenderness woven among its words, that it causes my heart to ache every time I read its timeless words.

Casting all your anxiety on Him, because He cares for you. (1 Peter 5:7)

You serve a God who cares about you. He cares about you intimately, exclusively, and passionately. Knowing His care is specifically aimed at you, are you obeying this thoughtful verse?

The word *casting* means to throw or hurl all your cares in one direction—toward the One who loves you beyond measure and who gave His very life for you. *Casting* in the Greek is *epiripto*, which is a compound word. "*Epi* means *upon*, as *on top of something.* The word *ripto* means *to hurl, to throw,* or *to cast,* and it often means *to violently throw* or *to fling something with great force.*"[22]

There is one other place in the New Testament where this strong, active word is used.

They brought it to Jesus, and they threw their coats on the colt and put Jesus on it. (Luke 19:35)

It is important to note that in secular literature at the time, *epiripto* was a word picture visualizing "the flinging of a garment, bag, or excess weight off the shoulders of a traveler and onto the back of some other beast, such as a donkey, camel, or horse."[23]

My friend, you were not made to carry the cares, worries, and anxieties of life on your shoulders or in your heart. But there is someone who can. Peter and the Holy Spirit are inviting you to violently and immediately throw the stress and worry of your life unto Jesus. He *is able* to carry your emotional burdens.

The word *cares* in Greek is *merimna*, which describes any anxiety, emotional affliction, difficulty, or hardship. These emotional challenges can be the result of relationship issues, physical challenges, financial stress, or anything else that brings concern to our minds and hearts.

How wonderful to know the reason we can *epiripto* our *merimna* upon Him is wrapped up in two little words: *He cares.* The Father is concerned about your life and interested in your day. He notices all those worries that have built up in your heart and He is inviting you to give to Him what is too burdensome for you to carry.

I don't share my heart or my concerns with those who don't care about me. God's care for me is infinite and spans the ages of eternity past. And so, I will cast all—not some but all—of my cares upon the One who cares all about me.

⧗ *List a few of the cares on your heart today.*

1. _____

2. _____

3. _____

THE MIRROR

⧗ *What happens to you when you try to carry objects too heavy for you? Now, what happens to you when you try to carry emotional challenges too heavy for you? What does it mean for you to know "He cares for you"?*

ETERNAL WORDS

Beloved, do not be surprised at the fiery ordeal among you, which comes upon you for your testing, as though some strange thing were happening to you; but to the degree that you share the sufferings of Christ, keep on rejoicing, so that also at the revelation of His glory you may rejoice with exultation. (1 Peter 4:12–13)

MY PRAYER FOR TODAY

Jesus, today I throw all of my cares upon You. I hurl every emotional item that causes me to worry upon You. And I resolve NOT to take them back. Thank You for caring for me. In Jesus' name I pray. Amen.

Day 5

Wake Up!

Have you ever overslept despite a clanging, loud alarm clock? Don't you feel out of sorts the rest of the day? I have missed important meetings, caused stress to my children, and made serious mistakes all because I refused to rouse myself from sleep in the early morning. It's not that I need a louder alarm clock—I just need better self-discipline.

Pay Attention!

Peter's alarm clock for the twenty-first-century church is intrusive and loud in the following verse:

> *Be of sober spirit, be on the alert. Your adversary, the devil, prowls around like a roaring lion, seeking someone to devour.* **(1 Peter 5:8)**

Peter is calling the children of God to wake up and be aware of what is happening in the world. We do have an enemy, his name is Satan, and his plan is dastardly and personal. He is the father of all lies. All persecution ultimately comes from his dark kingdom.

He is known by other pseudonyms as well: the devil, old Slewfoot, the accuser of the brethren, and Beelzebub. He hates God and he despises the people of God.

Although we need to stay uncommonly alert when it comes to the roar of the enemy, we can also know Satan only has force but no power. He only prowls about "like" a roaring lion. He was defanged by the price Jesus paid on Calvary's cross. His is a roar with no bite to it. The devil is pretending to be a roaring lion in a cheap and unconvincing costume.

What is true, however, is he is on the prowl, looking for someone to devour. That someone just might be you. Lions prey upon the weakest victim they can find. They attack the sick, the young, or straggling animals.

Lions always travel in pairs. One of the lions will roar at the defenseless prey from one side and that victim will turn and run in the other direction—straight into the jaws of the partner lion.

The enemy of the people of God employs this same technique in his attempt to be lion-like. He might roar "Cancer!" from one side, hoping you will run straight into the jaws of fear.

He roars, "That person hurt your feelings! They don't care about you!" In reaction, you turn and run directly into the path of unforgiveness, bitterness, and offense.

This lion of pretense loves to roar, "Bankruptcy! Poverty!" His victim then runs straight into the jaws of selfish living and decides, "I will no longer tithe. I can't afford it."

The enemy has been up to no good since the beginning of time. In the book of Job, the Lord had a conversation with Satan before he was allowed to attack the blameless and righteous, Job. Even then, during those ancient days, Satan was roaming the earth in his intimidating and delinquent fashion:

> *The Lord said to Satan, "From where do you come?" Then Satan answered the Lord and said, "From roaming about on the earth and walking around on it." (Job 1:7)*

On the other hand, the eyes of the Lord are looking for people on whom He can show His favor:

> *For the eyes of the Lord move to and fro throughout the earth that He may strongly support those whose heart is completely His. (2 Chronicles 16:9)*

⏳ *What are some practical disciplines you can incorporate into your life to stand strong against the enemy?*

1. _____

2. _____

3. _____

Resist

Peter's advice to a church in agonizing pain is as pertinent today as it was two thousand years ago.

> *But resist him, firm in your faith, knowing that the same experiences of suffering are being accomplished by your brethren who are in the world.* (1 Peter 5:9)

Your only hope of escape when meeting a lion in the jungle is if you have a quick-firing weapon in your hands. You do have such a weapon—the Word of God.

Declare the Word of God over your health, your finances, and your relationships. Shred the enemy with the two-edged sword of Scripture. I often remind women who are in a fierce battle to find a fighting verse and declare it loudly and often.

The next time you meet a lion in your daily routine, don't run away from him but stare him down. Don't flinch in his presence or he will be sure to attack. Resist him, firm in your faith, and he will be forced to slink away in defeat.

> *Submit therefore to God. Resist the devil and he will flee from you.* (James 4:7)

How wonderful to know Satan is not as powerful as the Lord. Remind yourself daily although the devil is prowling, he is certainly not more powerful than the mighty God we serve.

> *Because greater is He who is in you than he who is in the world.* (1 John 4:4)

⧖   *What exactly does it mean to "resist the devil and he will flee from you"?*

The Blessings of His Promise

After you have suffered for a little while, the God of all grace, who called you to His eternal glory in Christ, will Himself perfect, confirm, strengthen and establish you. (1 Peter 5:10)

Peter makes a promise on behalf of the Lord's grace, promising He is able to fill our hearts with joy and our lives with purpose. God has a nonnegotiable plan for His dear children. Even suffering is unable to destroy it.

The Lord is able to perfect or restore what has gone wrong in your life. He has the power and desire to put your life back in order after you have gone through personal pain or trauma. He truly is the God who works all things together for our good and His glory.

The Lord also has the authority and desire to provide a stable foundation for your life. He confirms that you are His. He wants to provide for you and give you an uncommon steadiness. He will support you with His Word, His wisdom, and His guidance.

How wonderful to know God will give you His strength when the storms of life have weakened you. The Lord provides His power to those who are battered and tired. He offers His courage to those who ask for it.

And finally, the Lord will establish you in all your ways. He will be your foundation and the Rock upon which you can build a wonderful life.

⧗ *I want you to take a minute and consider the following four words the Lord has spoken over your life. As you do, allow His undeniable presence to wash over you and accept His impartation of completion, stability, strength, and fortitude. Now, would you write a personal definition for each amazing word?*

Perfect

Confirm

Strengthen

Establish

To Him be dominion forever and ever. Amen. (**1 Peter 5:11**)

Our response to the overwhelming power and protection the Lord gives is a song of high praise and the joyful acknowledgement that He is the God of all power. We must never neglect our responsibility and delight to honor Him with worship and submission under His Lordship.

Just Ordinary People

Through Silvanus, our faithful brother (for so I regard him), I have written to you briefly, exhorting and testifying that this is the true grace of God. Stand firm in it! She who is in Babylon, chosen together with you, sends you greetings, and so does my son, Mark. Greet one another with a kiss of love.

Peace be to you all who are in Christ. (**1 Peter 5:12–14**)

Finally, Peter makes a list of ordinary people who are used in extraordinary times for the remarkable purposes of God. You and I are the ordinary people of this generation marked for the glorious cause of Christ. God cares about people, and He is keenly aware of how we choose to live during times of ease and during times of hardship.

Peter reminds all of God's people, in all the epochs yet to come, to stand firm in the true grace of God. His grace changes everything! Grace is the firm foundation upon which we build relationships, priorities, and our faith.

God's promise to you, even during the most difficult and demanding days of life, is His peace.

- When you don't like your life—God provides His amazing peace.
- When you are suffering yet trusting—the reward is God's incomparable peace.
- When you are taking care of the people to whom you are assigned—the benefit package includes God's miraculous peace.
- When you don't understand what you must endure—His promise to you is the peace that passes all understanding.

God's peace is the exclamation mark on every sentence of your life and the most precious aspect of all your days. The Father longs to give you His peace—regardless of circumstances. His peace is built on the full assurance that He is able to hold your life in the palm of His hand. When you throw your worries and troubles upon Him, He catches them all. Not one worry, not one piece of anxiety, and not one moment of stress passes by God. As He seizes your troubles and concerns—He throws His unshakable peace back to you.

THE MIRROR

⏳ *As we close our study of 1 Peter, what is one takeaway you hope to remember the rest of your life?*

ETERNAL WORDS

Beloved, do not be surprised at the fiery ordeal among you, which comes upon you for your testing, as though some strange thing were happening to you; but to the degree that you share the sufferings of Christ, keep on rejoicing, so that also at the revelation of His glory you may rejoice with exultation. (1 Peter 4:12–13)

MY PRAYER FOR TODAY

Father God, today I rejoice in Your faithfulness. I thank You for the promise that You will certainly perfect, confirm, strengthen, and establish me.

Use me, Father, at my moment in history just as you used Peter. Use my voice as a voice of encouragement and hope.

I commit to You, Lord, that I will "keep on rejoicing" every day of my life. In Jesus' name I pray. Amen.

NOTES

1. "Beowulf," Poetry Foundation, https://www.poetryfoundation.org/poems/43521/beowulf-old-english-version.

2. "Sonnet 3: Look in thy glass and tell the face thou viewest," Poetry Foundation, https://www.poetryfoundation.org/poems/50644/sonnet-3-look-in-thy-glass-and-tell-the-face-thou-viewest.

3. Roman historian Tacitus, "Nero's Persecution of the Christians," *The Annals*, Book XV; quoted from William Stearns Davis, *Readings in Ancient History: Illustrative Extracts from the Sources, vol. II. Rome and the West* (Boston: Allyn and Bacon, 1913), 287.

4. Rick Renner, *Sparkling Gems from the Greek: 365 New Gems to Equip and Empower You for Victory Every Day of the Year*, vol. 2 (Tulsa: Institute Books, 2017), 427.

5. James Strong, *Strong's Expanded Exhaustive Concordance of the Bible* (Nashville: Thomas Nelson, 2009), s.v. "eklektos," Blue Letter Bible.com, https://www.blueletterbible.org/lexicon/g1588/kjv/tr/0-1/.

6. William Barclay, *The Letters of James and Peter*, rev. ed. (Louisville: Westminster John Knox, 1976), 167.

7. Strong, *Strong's Concordance*, s.v. "charis," https://www.blueletterbible.org/lexicon/g5485/kjv/tr/0-1/.

8. Strong, *Strong's Concordance*, s.v. "zao," https://www.blueletterbible.org/lexicon/g2198/kjv/tr/0-1/.

9. Strong, *Strong's Concordance*, s.v. "parakyptō," https://www.blueletterbible.org/lexicon/g3879/kjv/tr/0-1/.

10. Strong, *Strong's Concordance*, s.v. "anazōnnymi," https://www.blueletterbible.org/lexicon/g328/nasb95/tr/0-1/.

11. Paul A. Cedar, *James, 1, 2 Peter, Jude*, vol. 11 of The Communicator's Commentary (Word Books, 1984), 125.

12. Cedar, *James, 1, 2 Peter, Jude*.

13. Reginald Heber, "Holy, Holy, Holy! Lord God Almighty," Hymnary.org, https://hymnary.org/text/holy_holy_holy_lord_god_almighty_early.

14. Reuben Morgan, "You Are Holy," track #6 on Hillsong Worship, *Touching Heaven Changing Earth*, 1998.

15. Rick Renner, *Sparkling Gems from the Greek: 365 Greek Word Studies for Every Day of the Year to Sharpen Your Understanding of God's Word*, vol. 1 (Tulsa: Teach All Nations, 2003), 202.

16. Strong, *Strong's Concordance*, s.v. "entimos," https://www.blueletterbible.org/lexicon/g1784/kjv/tr/0-1/.

17. Strong, *Strong's Concordance*, s.v. "pnîmâ," https://www.blueletterbible.org/lexicon/h6441/nasb95/wlc/0-1/.

18. Strong, *Strong's Concordance*, s.v. "exangellō," https://www.blueletterbible.org/lexicon/g1804/kjv/tr/0-1/.

19. Strong, *Strong's Concordance*, s.v. "exangellō," https://www.blueletterbible.org/lexicon/g1804/kjv/tr/0-1/.

20. Strong, *Strong's Concordance*, s.v. "exangellō," https://www.blueletterbible.org/lexicon/g1804/kjv/tr/0-1/.

21. Renner, *Sparkling Gems from the Greek*, vol. 1, 946.

22. Renner, *Sparkling Gems from the Greek*, vol. 1, 325.

23. Renner, *Sparkling Gems from the Greek*, vol. 1, 325.

www.ingramcontent.com/pod-product-compliance
Lightning Source LLC
Chambersburg PA
CBHW070022100426
42740CB00013B/2576